Bullion Bend

Confederate Stagecoach Robbers, Murder Trials, and the California Supreme Court — Oh My!

Authority Publishing
Gold River, California

Copyright © 2018 by William E. Cole. All rights reserved.

No part of this publication may be reproduced, stored in a retrieval system, or transmitted in any form or by any means, electronic, mechanical, photocopying, recording, scanning, or otherwise, without the prior written permission of the author.

Limit of Liability/Disclaimer of Warranty: While the publisher and author have used their best efforts in preparing this book, they make no representations or warranties with respect to the accuracy or completeness of the contents of this book and specifically disclaim any implied warranties of merchantability or fitness for a particular purpose. No warranty may be created or extended by sales representatives or written sales materials. The advice and strategies contained herein may not be suitable for your situation. You should consult with a professional when appropriate. Neither the publisher nor the author shall be liable for any loss of profit or any other commercial damages, including but not limited to special, incidental, consequential, personal, or other damages.

Bullion Bend: Confederate Stagecoach Robbers, Murder Trials, and the California Supreme Court – Oh My!

A riveting true story so amazing it needs to be a movie!

By William E. Cole

1. History/US/Civil War Period 2. True Crime/Heists & Robberies 3. History/US/State & Local/ West

ISBN: 978-1-935953-91-3 Hardcover
ISBN: 978-1-935953-90-6 Paperback
LCCN: 2018935357

Cover design by Lewis Agrell

Printed in the United States of America

Authority Publishing
11230 Gold Express Dr. #310-413
Gold River, CA 95670
800-877-1097
www.AuthorityPublishing.com

Dedication

This book is dedicated to my wife, Kristy. It's published in our forty-fifth year of marriage. Kristy is the love of my life, my partner, confident, spiritual guide, and friend. Without her patience and support, this book would not have made it to print.

ACKNOWLEDGMENTS

In acknowledging significant contributions, I apologize in advance if unintended oversights occur. A special word of thanks is due to Richard Williams, Eileen Short, and Sally Durst. As friends and cousins, their support and enthusiasm were instrumental to uncover some family history lost or long forgotten. Of course, I wouldn't be here without my brave pioneer relatives who traveled six months by wagon train to California in 1852, and my great-grandfather and great-grandmother who followed them via the transcontinental railroad in the early 1870s.

Also deserving acknowledgement are the hard-working newspaper reporters in 1864-65, who chronicled these amazing events during tumultuous times. They faithfully recorded and reported them to an eager reading public. Their painstakingly compiled details of the incredible and true events contained in this Wild West tale were invaluable for me to follow.

Right after I first discovered this epic story, I tracked down and contacted Richard Hughey. A retired columnist for the *Mountain Democrat* in Placerville, he wrote a series of columns about the escapades you will read about. Published as newspaper columns in late 1999 through early 2000, they contained many rich details worth their weight in gold. During our initial phone conversation in October 2015, we discussed my eagerness to deepen the breadth of understanding these events. He gave me permission and his blessing to freely utilize and draw upon the rich content contained in his columns. Thank you, Richard.

Two additional authors deserve special recognition and high praise. Dr. Robert J. Chandler, a retired Wells Fargo Bank historian is revered as the preeminent expert on Civil War California — this book's important time period. He sent me a packet of terrifically detailed information I had not seen published elsewhere. Thank you, Bob!

He referred me to author John Boessenecker. I previously read a well-researched and well-written chapter in his book, *Badges and Buckshot*, which contains details of this epic story. In my opinion, Boessenecker's work combined with Richard Hughey's columns are the most thorough and entertaining published accounts available. John's support went above and beyond what I could have expected. He willingly shared vintage photographs from his private collection. Thank you, John. I owe you an immense debt of gratitude.

To Authority Publishing — thank you. Ms. Stephanie Chandler and her staff have been great to work with for a second time! They went above and beyond to meet tight deadlines. Yes indeed, a very big thank you!

And finally, it's my privilege to acknowledge all the individuals who protect, provide access, and preserve the precious records and source documents in their care. Many people helped me discover documents, records, correspondence, and photographs directly related to telling this epic story. Specifically, let me thank the individuals and supporters of these fine institutions: the California State Archives, California State Library, History San Jose, Society of California Pioneers, Amador County Archives, and the El Dorado County Historical Museum.

Without these dedicated professionals and volunteers who staff archives, libraries, and repositories with a local, regional, statewide, national, or international reach, this book and many like it would never be written. They toil on our behalf and deserve our enormous debt of gratitude. Thank you!

Without you and the precious historical items you care for, they would be lost forever.

"If history and genealogy were taught in the form of stories, they would never be forgotten."

William E. Cole

CONTENTS

Dedication iii

Acknowledgments v

PROLOGUE

Preface 1

Introduction 3

Quest Begins 7

THE EPIC STORY

1 Brief California History Lesson 13

2 America's Growing Spirit of Disunity 19

3 Quantrill's Partisan Raiders, the Red Fox, and
   Preston Hodges 31

4 Stage is Set 45

5 Bullion Bend 53

6 Long Arm of the Law 61

7 Chase is On 69

8 Trials....................................... 85

9 Tribulations................................. 97

10 1865....................................... 111

11 Preston Hodges' Saga Concludes 123

Bibliography.................................. 133

Notes 139

Index 149

Bullion Bend

Confederate Stagecoach Robbers, Murder Trials, and the California Supreme Court — Oh My!

A riveting true story so amazing
it needs to be a movie!

PREFACE

Sound unbelievable? It might, but it's all true. Even the most creative mind would be hard-stretched to conjure up what's contained in this historical account. Eyewitness accounts testify to **facts stranger than fiction**.

The cast of real-life characters features California Confederates, Copperhead citizens, Civil War drama, court judges, and convicted criminals. The setting moves throughout California cities, courthouses, castles, jails, and prisons. This little-remembered piece of California history will stretch your imagination. It's a roller coaster ride filled with intrigue. With many twists and turns, these events made front page headlines for over a year. It's an epic story.

As you enjoy this daring-do tale, you will more deeply understand what California was like from statehood through the Civil War. You will discover the story and uncover the reasons that drew my relative into an intriguing web. It included a secret society, a daring stagecoach robbery, multiple court appearances, and . . . well . . . let's not give away the entire story yet.

Keep in mind it's all true. There's no need to make up dialogue or embellish the events. We can only again say, *Oh My!*

INTRODUCTION

As you start this amazing story, you should know two things. First, I'm a passionate genealogist — at it for nearly four decades. Second, I'm a third generation native Californian. For all but four and a half years of my entire life, I've lived in the Golden State. As the song lyrics say, "I love you, California. You're the greatest state of all."

However, California is, and always has been, a little different. As American author and essayist Edward Abbey once wrote: *There is science, logic, reason; there is thought verified by experience. And then there is California.*[1]

One night, an online search to fill in some gaps on my Hodges family yielded a surprising result. When this indexed record[2] popped up, I could only think, *What's this?*

> **ancestry**
>
> **Preston Hodges**
> in the California, Prison and Correctional Records, 1851-1950
>
> | | |
> |---:|:---|
> | Name: | Preston Hodges |
> | Birth Date: | abt 1831 |
> | Birth Place: | North Carolina |
> | Record Date: | 13 Sep 1864 |
> | Place of Crime: | El Dorado, California, USA |
> | Institution Place: | San Quentin, Marin, California, USA |
> | Age: | 33 |
>
> Source Citation
> California State Archives; Sacramento, California; Secretary of State California State Archives San Quentin Prison Registers

I thought, *Preston Hodges, born about 1831 in North Carolina. He sounds like mine. Record date is in 1864. That's the right timeframe. But my Preston lived in Santa Clara County — not El Dorado.* But the next line stopped me in my tracks. *Institution Place: San Quentin. That's the infamous state penitentiary!*

As the implications sank in, I thought, *Oh no — not in my family!* Followed quickly by, *Whoa! How can this possibly be true?*

Our Preston Hodges was a deeply committed Christian, he certainly wouldn't have committed a crime. Or would he? Then I remembered. Mom always said her side of the family was an ornery bunch!

Exactly who is Preston Hodges? He's in my mother's Williams line. He's my second great-granduncle, a brother of my second great-grandmother, Phoebe Hodges, who lived and died in Surry County, North Carolina.

INTRODUCTION

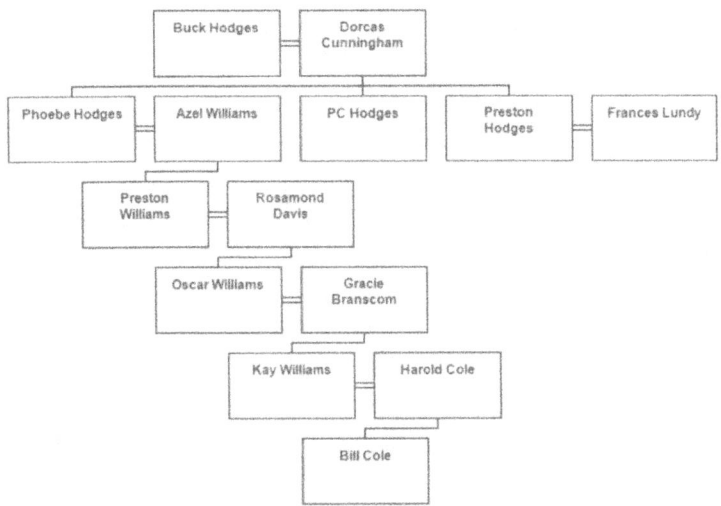

Intrigued, I asked myself, *Where is this record? It's at the California State Archives!* That's where this quest began. I knew I had to see the record for myself.

QUEST BEGINS

The California State Archives is a largely underutilized gem — a precious resource for our fine state's citizens. It was chartered by the California Legislature on January 5, 1850, nine months before statehood.

In passing the legislature's first law,[3] the state archive's charter was defined to "classify, and safely keep, and preserve . . . all records . . . connected with the political, civil, and military history, and past administration of the Government in California." Records included registers, maps, books, papers, tolls, documents, and other writings, on subjects "which may be interesting, or valuable as references of authorities to the Government, or people of the State."

One cool fall morning, I fed coins into a downtown Sacramento parking meter. As I hustled through the streets, my mental state anticipated what was about to happen. The prison record unearthed that fateful evening caused me to pause. It fanned my inquisitive nature. Could the archives record really be about my relative?

Upon arrival at 1020 O Street, I signed in at the security guard's desk. As I exited the elevator on the fourth floor, I filled out a form at the receptionist's station to indicate what I wanted to research. An archivist settled me in front of a microfilm reader. As she cued up the film for my review, she stayed with me in case I needed help.

The ledger's left side came into view first along the top of the page: "Register and Descriptive List of Convicts under Sentence of Imprisonment in the State Prison of California."[4] The first three entries, dated September 1, 1864, attracted our attention. Starting with 2817: Ah Shim, murder in the 2nd degree. 2818: Ah Foo, murder in the 2nd degree. 2819 Ah Sing, with ditto marks meaning the same date and same crime. All three prisoners were Chinese. I thought, *Is there a pattern here?* But the very next entry riveted my attention. 2820 listed Preston Hodges.

San Quentin Prison Register, Inmate No 2820, Preston Hodges
Courtesy of California State Archives, Sacramento

His nativity — North Carolina. He's put in the slammer on September 13, 1864. And those ditto marks again mean murder in the 2nd degree! His sentence is twenty years . . . yikes!!!

On the ledger's right side, more details emerged. This convicted felon is from El Dorado County. Since my Preston lived in Santa Clara County, that information did not match my relative. At age thirty-two, his occupation is a farmer. Since inmate photographs were not initiated until the 1880s, detailed features followed. This man is five feet nine with a florid complexion. His eyes are gray. He has sandy colored hair.

He's described with a high forehead, eyebrows projecting, and he's bald on the crown of his head. He's very much freckled on his arm, back, and shoulders. He's got three large moles on his back and a scar on the middle finger of his right hand. Another scar is on his left hand little finger. He's of medium build.

So far, there was no proof he was my Preston Hodges. He might be someone else with the same name.

The final remarks on the ledger's right side caught our attention. In much lighter ink, they are difficult to read. After much back and forth, we determined the phrase to read "pardoned by order of court, Feb'y 23, 1865."

We immediately dug deeper. The archivist unearthed other indexed references to Preston Hodges. One led to this file. It knocked my socks off: *People vs. Preston Hodges* — a California Supreme Court case!!![5]

Courtesy of Bill Cole collection

Really?

How would you feel to discover something like this — possibly about someone in your family tree? Surprised, embarrassed, at a loss for words? For me, it was all of those and more.

Have you ever had something grab a hold of you and not let go? That's exactly what happened to me. I was hooked. I knew I needed to get to the bottom of this. I committed to do the work necessary to find out the truth.

What started as a simple exercise to fill in some missing genealogical information became an all-consuming quest to find out the real story. As I delved deeply into the archives records and other historical accounts, I found much more than I bargained for.

Did you know about California Confederate secret societies in operation during the Civil War?

No? Neither did I! Let's begin with a brief California history lesson.

1
BRIEF CALIFORNIA HISTORY LESSON

This 1849 vintage photograph[6] shows the community affectionately known as Hangtown. It's located just nine miles from Sutter's Mill in Coloma — the epicenter of California's Gold Rush.

Just the year prior, the event that changed history was best described by James W. Marshall.[7]

While we were in the habit at night of turning the water through the tail race we had dug for the purpose of widening and deepening the race, I used to go down in the morning to see what had been done by the water through the night; and about half past seven o'clock on or about the 19th of January — I am not quite certain to the day, but it was between the 18th and the 20th of that month — 1848, I went down as usual, and after shutting off the water from the race I

Old Hangtown c1849 (05608)
Courtesy of El Dorado County Historical Museum

stepped into it, near the lower end, and there, upon the rock, about six inches beneath the surface of the water, I DISCOVERED THE GOLD.

I was entirely alone at the time. I picked up one or two pieces and examined them attentively; and having some general knowledge of minerals, I could not call to mind more than two which in any way resembled this — sulphuret of iron, very bright and brittle; and gold, bright, yet malleable; I then tried it between two rocks, and found that it could be beaten into a different shape, but not broken.

I then collected four or five pieces and went up to Mr. Scott (who was working at the carpenter's bench making the mill wheel) with the pieces in my hand and said, 'I have found it.'

BRIEF CALIFORNIA HISTORY LESSON

Scott inquired, 'What is it?' 'Gold,' I answered. Replied Scott, 'That can't be.' I said, 'I know it to be nothing else.'

Marshall's phrase, "I have found it," is translated from the Greek word "eureka." EUREKA! became the cry of gold miners throughout the Mother Lode when they struck it rich in the land of El Dorado!

A few months earlier, store owner Sam Brannan set up shop at Sutter's Fort in Sacramento. When rumors of Marshall's gold strike surfaced, Brannan headed to the mines to see for himself if it was true. Convinced there was *more gold than all the people in California could take out in fifty years,* he planned a second store and traveled to San Francisco in May.

When Brannan stepped off the ferry, he swung his hat, lifted and waved a quinine bottle full of gold, and yelled, *Gold! Gold! Gold! Gold from the American River!* Within a month, the majority of males left town and headed for *them thar (sic) hills* to make their fortune.

On December 5, 1848, President James Polk announced in his State of the Union letter that reports of California gold were true. The gold rush was on!

On September 9, 1850, California became the thirty-first state, with Eureka as its state motto. It was the first state admitted to the Union that was not a colony or territory prior to statehood. Why was that? If you were the government, would you want your hands on all that gold? Certainly!

BUT HISTORY IS RARELY THAT SIMPLE. THE FACT IS THAT CALIFORNIA BECAME A STATE NOT JUST FOR THE GOLD. THE OTHER FACTOR RESOLVED A CONTROVERSY AND TEST OF POLITICAL WILL.

As Congress debated California's admittance beginning in 1849, Kentucky's Senator Henry Clay introduced resolutions in January of 1850 designed to avert a crisis between the North and South over slavery. Five congressional actions included California's admittance to the Union as a free state. Collectively, they became known as the Compromise of 1850.[8]

In 1850, state borders along and east of the Mississippi River were essentially the same as today. But further west, there was a wide swatch of open land before you arrived in California. In that year's census, California's total population was 92,597 residents. Of the original twenty-seven counties formed at statehood, the five most prominent counties each counted a sparse residents' population.

SAN FRANCISCO	21,000
EL DORADO	20,057
SACRAMENTO	9,087
SANTA CLARA –RECORDS LOST, ESTIMATED	5,000
LOS ANGELES	1,610

For the next few years, cries of "Eureka!" echoed throughout the Mother Lode. A few struck it rich. Most did not.

In 1850, Preston Hodges married Frances Lundy in Surry County, North Carolina. Lured by tales of the golden state's riches. Preston, age nineteen, and his wife arrived in California in November of 1852. By then, Frances Hodges was sixteen and six months pregnant.

They were accompanied by her two brothers, David and Daniel Lundy, plus Preston's brother, Pleasant Cunningham Hodges, the eldest son of the Buck Hodges and Dorcas Cunningham Hodges. Known as P.C., he was the wagon master. The Hodges and Lundy families' entry into California was quite memorable.

Frances Lundy Hodges
Courtesy of Sally Durst collection

After six months of arduous travel from Missouri, the wagon train crossed over the Sierra Nevada mountains late, racing to beat the snowfall. Chased by Native American Indians, they witnessed the devastation of Sacramento's great fire, and experienced a legendary flood. That story called, *Welcome to California*, we'll save for another time!

The Hodges and Lundy siblings arrived at the gold rush's peak — history's largest mass migration. The state's population soared. In 1852, just two years after the 1850 census, 260,249 people from all walks of life were living in California — a growth rate of one hundred and eighty-one percent.

The easy "pickins" of gold began to peter out in 1856. During a recession in 1857, P.C. Hodges went back to his North Carolina home for a family visit and told stories of

California and the El Dorado. His brother-in-law, Azariah Lundy, wrote in his diary.[9]

> *PC Hodges come to Cal in 1850 and come back to NC in 1857 and while sitting around a big fire place . . . and hearing young PC Hodges tell his experience of the north west of the free soil of one hundred and sixty acres of land by take a homested (sic) on it in any of the Western States or territories and level good ritch (sic) soil . . . and I was only 16 years old — it filled my bosom with bright prospects for the future and the stories he told me about Cal and the gold he had taked (sic) out of the mines.*

Most certainly, this author's nine-year-old great-grandfather, Preston Williams, sat listening to P.C. along with Azariah Lundy at that same big fireplace. They both later followed their two Hodges' uncles, P.C. and Preston, to California.

2
AMERICA'S GROWING SPIRIT OF DISUNITY

The Compromise of 1850 did not settle the lightning rod issue of slavery. Extremist positions ignited dissension on all sides. Throughout the decade, a brewing cauldron of dissent revealed a growing disunity in the United States. There was no abate in the debate whether in the North, South, East, or West.

California's gold rush created an ethnically-diverse population right from the state's birth. As the population growth continued, ten percent of California's total population was thought to support Confederate causes even though California was officially a Union state. That equated to 40,000 Southern sympathizers by 1860.

On July 4, 1854, in Ohio, Dr. George W. L. Bickley founded the Knights of the Golden Circle (KGC). Author David C. Keehn wrote about the KGC: *The Knights were a militant oath-bound secret society dedicated to promoting southern rights (including slavery) and extending American hegemony over the Golden Circle region. Membership was open to all southern men of good character as well as northern men who stood by the constitutional claims of the South.*[10]

KGC's constitution advocated states seceding from the Union if, in their eyes, it ever became necessary. The knights used secret signs, passwords, and handshakes. They operated from castles, really! After all, knights need castles, don't they? At least that's what they called them — although most were simple farms!

But KGC founder Bickley cast an even larger vision for the organization. He envisioned the Golden Circle region as a slave-holding empire that encircled the Southern states, Mexico, Central America, the northern parts of South America, and the entire Caribbean region with Havana as its capital.

KGC support spread rapidly throughout California. Strong contingents operated in Los Angeles, San Bernardino, El Monte, Visalia, and San Jose, the Santa Clara County seat. Which is exactly where Preston Hodges lived and ranched.

In 1858 when silver was discovered in Nevada, an economic recovery began. Governor John B. Weller privately envisioned an independent Pacific Republic with California, Oregon, and others. In 1859, the legislature, which was viewed as intensely pro-slavery, passed the Pico Act. Legislators asked Congress to divide the state into North and South California.

But California's most important 1859 event wasn't even in the state. The discovery of the richest silver mine ever — the Comstock Lode in Virginia City, Nevada — set in motion events dramatically effecting California's future. Let's set the scene.

Do you remember the hit 1960s television show *Bonanza*? Television reruns are still featured today. Its fictional main characters — Adam, Little Joe, Hoss, and Ben Cartwright — became household names. Can you hum the opening music theme song? There's good odds you can! The closest town to the Cartwright clan's home, the Ponderosa Ranch, was Virginia City. Memorable fictional characters such as the cook, Hop Sing, and Sheriff Roy Coffey rounded out a stellar cast of characters.

Times boomed in Virginia City, Nevada. Shipments of silver bullion and bags of gold dust left daily for the El Dorado. A new reporter, Samuel Clemens, wrote for the local newspaper. His pen name was Mark Twain.

The adjacent California county, El Dorado, was the place to make a fortune. With town names like "Mother Lode," "Mud Springs," and "Rough and Ready," well you get the picture. In 1854, El Dorado's county seat was renamed Placerville from "Hangtown." That moniker aptly described its legendary approach to lawlessness. The town fathers re-branded its image for obvious reasons. The town's original name, "Old Dry Diggins" was changed at the gold rush's very beginning.

The silver boom in Nevada advanced what the gold rush started. In fact, silver fueled the growth and wealth of San Francisco even more than gold.

By the 1860 census, California's population dramatically increased to 379,974 residents now divided into forty-five counties. In the preceding decade, the population count in California's five most prominent counties grew to new levels.

SAN FRANCISCO	56,802
EL DORADO	20,562
SACRAMENTO	24,142
SANTA CLARA	11,962
LOS ANGELES	4,365

On the national stage, four presidential candidates emerged: Abraham Lincoln of the recently-formed Republican Party,

Northern Democrat Stephen Douglas, Southern Democrat John C. Breckinridge, and John Bell who represented the Constitutional Union Party. Except for Lincoln, the rest were in favor of various shades of status quo. When Lincoln won his party's nomination in March, it created the most contentious presidential campaign ever. Even when compared to recent campaign experiences!

During the campaign, Lincoln addressed slavery as a moral issue. His platform advocated prohibiting slavery in territories and containing slavery to where it already existed. Stephen Douglas mainly avoided the slavery issue. His platform opposed the federal slave code in territories and supported popular sovereignty.

John Breckinridge supported the federal slave code in territories and supported popular sovereignty. John Bell avoided the slavery issue totally and advocated keeping the country united.

Predictably, the Democratic and independent candidates splintered support, while Lincoln's astute political savvy recognized the growing importance of the West. His platform included the proposed Homestead Act and financial support for the Transcontinental Railroad.

On November's election day, the popular vote split between the four candidates. Lincoln received less than 40% of the total popular vote . . . hardly a mandate. In California, he was even less popular with only 32.3% of the vote.

AS WE KNOW FROM RECENT ELECTIONS, THE POPULAR VOTE IS NOT WHAT ELECTS THE PRESIDENT. WHAT COUNTS IS THE ELECTORAL COLLEGE VOTES.

As expected, the Southern states voted as a bloc for Breckinridge. Missouri was the only state Douglas won outright. Four Northern states bordering the Mississippi

River — Illinois, Wisconsin, Minnesota, and Iowa, awarded their combined twenty-four electoral votes to Lincoln.

Out west in Oregon, Lincoln squeaked by with 270 votes more than Breckinridge. That enabled him to win three electoral votes with only 36.2% of the popular vote.

And in California, Lincoln won pluralities in only nine of the forty-five California counties. But — it was just enough . . . enabling his win of four electoral votes.

Without winning the thirty-one electoral college votes in the North's westernmost states, Lincoln would have fallen just short of the required 152 votes to win the election outright. God only knows what would have happened if the election was decided in the House of Representatives.

Lincoln won 180 electoral votes. Three other candidates split the remaining electoral college votes: Breckinridge — 72; Bell — 39; and Douglas — 12.

The election's aftermath was swift. In rapid order, seven states seceded from the Union.

DECEMBER 20	SOUTH CAROLINA
JANUARY 9	MISSISSIPPI
JANUARY 10	FLORIDA
JANUARY 11	ALABAMA
JANUARY 19	GEORGIA
JANUARY 26	LOUISIANA
FEBRUARY 1	TEXAS

On February 11, 1861, in Springfield, Illinois, president-elect Lincoln embarked on a seventy-city whistle-stop train tour. A scheduled stop in Baltimore on February 23 would precede his arrival in Washington DC prior to his March 4 inauguration.

Upon hearing unsubstantiated rumors, railroad officials hired Allan Pinkerton to investigate suspicious activities along

Lincoln's route through Baltimore. Convinced an alleged KGC assassination plot to stab the president-elect in Baltimore was real, Pinkerton ordered extraordinary security precautions. He changed schedules, trains, and cut telegraph lines to Baltimore on the evening of February 22.

A special train pulled into a downtown Baltimore station in the middle of the night. It carried a disguised Abraham Lincoln. A local downtown ordinance required trains to be horse-drawn between two stations during those hours. Quietly and secretly Lincoln passed through the city. Lincoln arrived in Washington DC undisturbed on February 23.

The large Baltimore crowd assembled at the train station for the president-elect's arrival grew impatient and increasingly restless. When they found out Lincoln passed through town incognito, the press skewered Lincoln unmercifully for his perceived cowardly act.

Years later in 1934, two boys discovered a cache of 5,000 gold coins buried in a Baltimore basement. Could this treasure have been designated by KGC to pay for the assassination attempt?[11] Perhaps, but we may never know for sure. The treasure's discovery location was just four blocks from where a known member of the KGC Baltimore castle lived. His name was John Wilkes Booth.

In California, secessionists supported the rebellion by joining KGC and other like organizations. Their collective goal was to provide local Confederacy assistance. The total estimated number of California secessionists ranged from five to sixteen thousand individuals. There are accounts that range even higher — from twenty to forty thousand individuals. Retired Wells Fargo historian and pre-eminent California Civil War expert, Dr. Robert J. Chandler, believes that inflated estimates may have been politically motivated.

In San Francisco's KGC castle, a "Band of 30" emerged out of the organization's highest order — the 3rd Degree Knights of the Columbian Star. These wealthy patrons wielded powerful political influence. The Band of 30 was reputedly headed by United States Senator William Gwin. Born in Mississippi, he was one of California's first two US senators along with John C. Fremont. Many have never been identified. Estimates of KGC knights in California range from hundreds to thousands. No one knows for sure. Remember, it was a secret society. One source states, "By the spring of 1861 . . . the Knights of the Golden Circle was well-established in California."[12]

This KGC group plotted to take control of San Francisco and the Bay Area to divert gold shipments destined for the North to the Confederacy via Texas to significantly impede any Union war effort. Their elaborate plan included seizure of the Presidio, US Mint, custom house, Fort Point, Alcatraz, Benecia's arsenal, and other federal properties. They also intended to seize the state government in Sacramento.

In a stroke of good fortune and timing for Union loyalists, Brigadier General Edwin Sumner arrived on April 24 at San Francisco's Presidio. Sumner's orders were to replace the Commander of the Pacific, General Albert Sidney Johnson — a known Southern sympathizer loyal to Texas. He had already been recalled by the War Department.

General Sumner's arrival caused the KGC's scheme to fall apart before a cataclysmic event became widely known in San Francisco. In fact, a Pony Express rider arrived the very same day, April 24, with news that might have fueled the Southern sympathizers' elaborate plan. Just two weeks earlier on April 12, Confederate canons opened fire at Fort Sumter which guarded Charleston Harbor in South Carolina. After two days of heavy bombardment, on April 14, the Union fort's commander, Major Robert Anderson, had no choice but to surrender. God only knows how this event's news might have affected the resolve of San Francisco Confederate patriots.

General Sumner knew of General Johnston's San Francisco

secessionist conspirators. Within four days of Sumner's arrival on April 28, he wrote to the Army Adjutant General and disclosed:

> *The secessionists are much the most active and zealous party, which gives them more influence than they ought to have from their numbers. I have no doubt that there is some deep scheming to draw California into the secessionist movement, in the first place as the Republic of the Pacific, expecting afterwards to induce her to join the Southern Confederacy."*
> He then warned the War Department that *"the troops now here will hold their positions, but if there should be a general uprising of the people, they could not . . . put it down.*[13]

Back in the nation's capital after Fort Sumter's fall, Lincoln immediately met the crisis head on. He needed to mobilize the federal government for war. With less than 800 officers and 14,000 enlisted men, the US Army was dramatically understaffed for what lay ahead.

Lincoln used the only available law, the Militia Act of 1792. It empowered the president to call out the militia to suppress an insurrection. On April 15, Lincoln issued a proclamation declaring that an insurrection existed. He called out 75,000 men to put it down.

Lincoln asked the highest ranking American general and military hero, General Winfield Scott, who should command the Union Army. Winfield did not hesitate in his recommendation. He knew the right man for the job — a man he personally mentored.

At the time, the most decorated soldier in the US Army was a top-of-his-class West Point graduate. He fought with distinction in the Mexican-American War. He had served as Superintendent at West Point. He disagreed with slavery and believed that secession was unwise. Recently promoted to Colonel, he had devoted his life to serving the United States of America.

This decorated military officer wrote, *I can anticipate no greater calamity for the country than a dissolution of the Union. It would be an accumulation of all the evils we complain of, and I am willing to sacrifice everything but honor for its preservation.*[14]

GENERAL SCOTT KNEW WHO SHOULD COMMAND THE UNION ARMY. THE RIGHT MAN WAS AN OBVIOUS CHOICE. HE RECOMMENDED ROBERT E. LEE.

Previously, the Confederate States Army offered Lee command. He ignored it. On General Scott's recommendation, Lincoln quickly promoted Lee to Major General and offered him the command of the Union Army. But Lee's home state, Virginia, seceded on April 17, 1861.

On the evening of April 19, Robert E. Lee decided to resign his US Army commission and wrote two letters. One letter notified the Secretary of War of his decision. The second informed his commanding officer and mentor, General Winfield Scott, why he decided to turn down Lincoln's offer. General Scott said, *Lee, you have made the greatest mistake of your life.*[15]

However, in Lee's mind, it was a straightforward choice. He viewed himself as a Virginian more than an American. He followed his state, even though he personally disagreed with it. He viewed his service to the South not as a fight against the Union, but as a defense of Virginia. Lee once wrote, *I shall never bear arms against the Union, but it may be necessary for me to carry a musket in the defense of my native state, Virginia, in which case I shall not prove recreant to my duty.*[16]

On April 19, Lincoln issued another proclamation blockading Southern ports.[17] It provided that, "a competent force will be posted . . . to prevent entrance and exit of vessels" from the ports of the states in rebellion.

He authorized "the Secretary of State to affix the Seal of the United States to a Proclamation setting on foot a Blockade of the ports of the States of South Carolina, Georgia, Alabama, Florida, Mississippi, Louisiana, and Texas." Announced that day, the seal was affixed to the blockade proclamation — a de facto declaration of war by the Union against the Confederacy. The War Between the States was official. The Civil War had begun. In the North, it was also known as the War of the Rebellion. But in the South, it was known as the War of Northern Aggression.

Three more Southern states seceded: Arkansas on May 6; North Carolina on May 20; and Tennessee on June 8. Patriotism in the north and south bred volunteers. Both sides mobilized for protracted military engagements. Skirmishes increased during the last half of 1861.

As the war progressed, the Knights of the Golden Circle's importance diminished. After Bickley was removed as its head in 1860, he continued to recruit knights. In late 1861, when KGC sought to supply enough soldiers for a planned invasion of Mexico, they failed miserably. In San Francisco, the political will gained steam for Union causes. But ardent Southern sympathizers continued faithfully to support their cause.

In 1862, skirmishes intensified dramatically and transformed into major battles. Strong convictions on both sides led to fierce fighting between the armies of the Union and the Confederacy. Five bloody battles became indelibly etched into our collective national consciousness. In just seventeen fighting days, more than 7,000 soldiers per day were either killed, wounded, or missing in action. The casualties totaled more than 120,000 men.

APRIL 6-7	SHILOH
JUNE 25-JULY 1	SEVEN DAYS BATTLE
AUGUST 28-30	BULL RUN
SEPTEMBER 17	ANTIETAM
DECEMBER 11-15	FREDERICKSBURG

With advanced equipment available, photographers including Matthew Brady had unprecedented access to the war. Their coverage brought war's realism to mainstream America. For the first time in history, the public saw horrific war scenes up close and personal.

When photographs were displayed in major northern cities, people lined up for hours to see dead bodies. Real-life photos of the war's horrors elicited gut-wrenching emotions. Imagine how family members felt when the War Department soldiers knocked on their doors.

Throughout this era, Confederate supporters were increasingly labeled as "Copperheads." This term meant "snakes that strike silently." It was broadly applied and fueled the nation's deep divisions. This was particularly true in California, even though the war battles were far away.

In an article about these turbulent times, Dr. Chandler noted that in September of 1862: *The army banned papers from the mails in Los Angeles, Placerville, San Jose, Stockton, and Visalia as well as several towns in Oregon. It imprisoned five men whom local Unionists found too vocal. Prisoners came from Benecia, Los Angeles, Sacramento, and Visalia, and to house some, the army constructed the first prison building on its secure Bay fortification, Alcatraz.*[18] The publisher of the *Mountain Democrat* in Placerville was D.W. Gelwicks. He was widely regarded as a Copperhead. His newspaper was one refused postal privileges.

Published February 28, 1863, a political cartoon captured the essence of the North's prevailing views.

Courtesy of Library of Congress. LC-USZ62-132749[19]

The war's carnage intensified further in 1863. In the seven days between April 30-May 6, the battle of Chancellorsville resulted in 29,000 casualties — more than 4,100 soldiers per day.

And then, Gettysburg started on July 1. Even today, the brutal battle's total casualties are unknown. Total estimates exceed 50,000 soldiers in just three days. That's more than 16,600 soldiers per day. That's five-plus 9-11's!

NO OTHER WAR, FOREIGN OR OTHERWISE, HAS EVER APPROACHED THE VERACITY AND FEROCITY OF AMERICANS FIGHTING AMERICANS.

When Gettysburg finally ended on July 3rd, it was judged a tactical draw. In retrospect, it's recognized as the war's turning point in favor of the Union. But the South's demise was not the prevailing sentiment — particularly for Confederate sympathizers.

3

QUANTRILL'S PARTISAN RANGERS, THE RED FOX, AND PRESTON HODGES

Just seven weeks after Gettysburg, Captain William Clarke Quantrill assembled three hundred fifty members of his Confederate Partisan Rangers. In addition, one hundred Confederate Army recruits joined him under the command of Col. John D. Holt.

Quantrill's rangers included Frank and Jesse James, Cole Younger and his brother, "Bloody Bill" Anderson, and George Todd. None were commissioned in the Confederate States Army (CSA).

According to eyewitnesses, Captain Rufus Harvey Ingram was also present even though he's not listed on Quantrill's rosters. Known as the "Red Fox," he held a CSA Captain's commission.

Red Fox Ingram was about thirty years old. He stood five feet ten inches tall with blue eyes and dark hair. From Missouri, he weighed about one hundred and fifty pounds with long whiskers. Two years later, a California sheriff[20] regarded him as *a decidedly superior man for a desperado.* He labeled him a man of *coolness, sagacity, and an indomitable will* with a good education and *easy, suave, magnetic manners.*

His presence with Quantrill suggests Ingram liaised for Confederate Gen. Sterling Price, Quantrill's commanding officer. Price was believed to be KGC.

On August 21, 1863, Quantrill's Rangers rode into Lawrence, Kansas. The resulting raid turned into a five-hour rampage. They burned one hundred and eighty-five buildings and killed one hundred and eighty men and boys who might have been called to Union military service. Many wives and mothers heroically tried to save their fathers, sons, and husbands. That day, eighty women became widows, and one hundred children were orphaned.

Afterwards, the raiders escaped to Texas. When "Bloody Bill" Anderson rebelled, Quantrill's gang feuded and split. Red Fox Ingram fled to Mexico City. Late in 1863, he met Californian George Baker in a cantina. A Southern sympathizer, Baker was on his way east to join the Confederate Army.

Baker told Ingram about a KGC castle in Santa Clara County. The knights were trying to organize guerrilla activity but lacked a capable field leader. Baker thought Ingram could provide that leadership. He suggested they both go there to conduct partisan raids. Enticed, Ingram agreed. A relative, John Ingram, lived there. As did Preston Hodges.

Preston and Frances Hodges raised their family on a hillside ranch near Milpitas. In the picturesque mountains east of San Jose, the Arroyo Hondo was nearby.

After their firstborn daughter's death in Missouri, they celebrated their first California-born child, Sarah, in 1853. Joseph was born in 1854, Alice in 1855, and Clara in 1857. In 1858, Joseph died at age four. William was born in 1859

Frances and Preston Hodges, c 1860s
Courtesy of Sally Durst collection

and named for Preston's father. Daughter Frances followed in 1862.

Preston prospered in ranching. Well-respected and esteemed in his community, his upbringing grounded him in the Baptist faith. A devout Christian, he led his family daily to what he called "the family altar" — where they studied Scripture together.

Remember the sixteen-year-old Azariah Lundy, the brother of Preston's wife, Frances? In 1857, Azariah sat at the North Carolina campfire enthralled by his uncle PC's California. In his diary,[21] he asked his uncle, PC Hodges, to loan him money to come to California. He promised he'd work it off. PC Hodges gave him a deadline to pursue his dream: March 26, 1858.

On that exact date, young Azariah set off to follow his burning desire. He worked his way west to Jackson County, Missouri, arriving a year later. He then worked for Sam Boyd and a young man named Morris whose rented farm failed.

In the fall of 1860, Azariah Lundy rode for the Pony Express from Council Grove, Kansas, to Fort Pawnee directly through the Cow Indian territory. Azariah then soldiered in Mexico, Santa Fe, Arizona, and "over the county" in 1863. When discharged from Fort Leavenworth, he left for California on the sixth of May, 1863, just three months prior to Quantrill's raid.

In November of 1863, Azariah Lundy arrived at the Hodges ranch belonging to his brother-in-law and sister. He carried news from Missouri and back home in North Carolina. According to author J.G. Kearney, *There is no doubt Azariah's tales of circumstances happening in Missouri and the wester theater of the Civil War fueled Preston's ambition to offer aide in some way to his relative's defense. The family 'back home' were facing a demolition of their lives.*[22]

On March 23, 1864, Frances Hodges gave birth to another daughter, Elizabeth, nicknamed Lizzie. The family now numbered eight. This same month, Abraham Lincoln promoted Ulysses S. Grant to Commanding General of the Union Army.

In May of 1864, Grant moved his army towards Richmond, Virginia, and began the war of attrition against Lee's Northern Virginia Army. Union troops invaded Georgia from Chattanooga, Tennessee, and started the Atlanta campaign.

As the war raged on, newspaper reports kept Preston well-informed of the ongoing battles and terrible tragedies.

> EVEN SO, IT'S DOUBTFUL THAT PRESTON HODGES
> ANTICIPATED THE UNFOLDING EVENTS DRAWING HIM
> DEEPLY INTO A WEB OF SECRECY AND INTRIGUE.

RED FOX ARRIVES IN CALIFORNIA

In the spring of 1864, Red Fox Ingram and George Baker arrived in the Santa Clara valley. They immediately sought out a KGC castle meeting, where Captain Ingram presented his CSA commission.[23]

Another experienced KGC knight since the war's beginning, Thomas Bell Poole,[24] caught the attention of Red Fox. At six feet tall, this rough-looking Kentucky widower singly raised three children on his Pajaro River ranch near Watsonville in Santa Cruz County.

Poole served as a popular Monterey County undersheriff from 1858-60. He was a strong-willed take-charge officer.

Tom Poole, *Courtesy of John Boessenecker collection*

One of Poole's first official undersheriff acts created a controversial firestorm. Jose Anastasio cut a man's throat and robbed him of nine dollars. Convicted of murder, his death sentence scheduled his hanging for February 12, 1858.

After technical reporting oversights by the Monterey County Court, Governor Weller sent a reprieve to delay his execution until March 5. Unfortunately, the name listed on the Governor's executive order[25] was Anastasio Jesus — not Jose Anastasio.

Poole consulted with a local attorney and a court judge. He wanted to cover his rear end. Did the name's misspelling contained in the Governor's order invalidate it? Satisfied with the counsel he received, Poole proceeded constructing temporary gallows located right where the murder occurred. On a hill between Carmel and Monterey, the gallows made a very visible statement to the public! Precisely on schedule, he carried out the execution before a large crowd by stringing up Anastasio on February 12.

When news of this execution reached the governor's office, a staffer wrote across this original executive order[26] in big red letters: *This person was hung by Deputy Sheriff Poole in violation of this order.*[27]

An enraged Governor Weller wrote to Poole.[28] *You are guilty of judicial murder,* Weller charged. He added, *Your name ought to be consigned to eternal infamy.*

Poole responded by letter to the governor.[29] He reasoned that, if he did not hang Anastasio, the citizens probably would have created a public furor in his county. He declared, *My duty was plain; a ministerial officer has no duty to correct the errors of process, not to shield even the Governor from the legal results of a blunder.*

Poole blasted the governor with unparalleled language: *If there be difficulty and wrong in this matter, you are the culpable party . . . Not all your pompous but puerile ebulitions, nor the*

Governor's Reprieve Entry for Jose Anastasio, 1858
Courtesy of the California State Archives, Sacramento

vapid slang of a few slimy and venal journals which essay to be your mouthpieces, have shaken confidence in the rectitude of my course.

Imagine Poole writing this and thinking: *If your vocabulary, Governor Weller, is broad enough to understand my message — take that!* Holy mackerel, oh my!

Finally, a newspaper report[30] quoted Thomas Poole's poetic waxing aimed at Governor Weller. *A cur may bay the moon and feel chagrinned that the luminary does not fall at his feet; but reasonable men offer him no sympathy. The experience of the world shows that ambition often overleaps itself, and incompetence regrets its weakness; yet it is well, sometimes, that that power be not vested in a hand likely to abuse it.*[31]

Another of Poole's major KGC escapades happened on March 14, 1863. In San Francisco Bay, he participated in an elaborate scheme to commandeer a ship on behalf of the Confederacy. Arrested and charged with treason, he was imprisoned at Fort Alcatraz.

Seven months later, Poole swore an oath of allegiance to the United States and posted a bond of $3,000 to gain his freedom. Based on his subsequent actions, he had no intention of abandoning his Copperhead roots.

RED FOX IMMEDIATELY CHOSE THOMAS BELL POOLE AS HIS SECOND IN COMMAND. IN THE SPRING OF 1864, THEY FORMED THE LEADERSHIP NUCLEUS OF WHAT BECAME "CAPT. INGRAM'S PARTISAN RANGERS" — THE AREA'S KGC MILITARY UNIT.

KGC meetings were held at a redwood forested camp just west of San Jose. High above the town of Saratoga in the Santa Cruz mountains, some fifty San Jose sympathizers and Copperheads secretly discussed plans to support the Confederacy. According to one source, KGC "members were supposed to pay an initiation fee of one dollar and a weekly tax of ten cents."[32]

Initial discussions included guerrilla activity against the federal government. Red Fox Ingram proposed a raid on San Jose community banks planned to raise money to recruit and equip men to fight for the Confederacy in Texas under his command.

When Red Fox Ingram arrived, George Cross was already a knight. Cross, a well-known pioneer who had come to California with Fremont, took part in the 1846 Bear Flag revolt and made a small fortune panning for gold in 1848.

James Grant was also a knight. Grant was a known scoundrel and *randy punk with a big mouth and quick fists.*[33] Grant also fancied himself a ladies' man. In fact, it's believed a fight between Cross and Grant's girl caused him to leave the group.

Cross apparently feared for his life and took a room with a local farmer named Hogan. Without thinking, he revealed Ingram's plot to rob banks and kill any citizens who got in the way.

Hogan reported it to Sheriff John Hicks Adams who plotted to ambush Ingram's rangers. He asked Undersheriff R. B. Hall to spy on the knights' castle meeting.

When Hall uncovered the KGC castle meeting location near Saratoga, he staked it out. His intent was simply to spy and take notes. When he saw two dozen prominent valley merchants, famers, and ranchers assemble for the camp's meeting, he hastily scribbled a few notes: *All Democrats*.[34] Years later, Hall published a colorful story about this episode.[35]

> *They had selected an unusually secluded spot, the spur of the mountain protecting them on one side from the view of the village, while the thick pines and chaparral hid them completely on the other. I settled myself in a comfortable position, from whence I could command a view of the whole company, grasped my sixshooter and waited.*
>
> *Pretty soon they began to gather by twos and threes, until quite a crowd had collected, and, sure enough, it was just as I had suspected, the Knights of the Golden Circle, and among them some of the most prominent men in San Jose!*

KGC knights and sympathizers most likely in attendance besides Red Fox Ingram included John Ingram, Tom Poole, John A. Robertson (a local secessionist and San Jose storekeeper), George Cross, and James Grant. Other knights and partisan raiders included: "John and Wallace Clendenning; John Creal Bouldware, a San Jose carpenter; James Wilson, a young blacksmith from Missouri; Henry Ignatius Jarboe; Joseph W. Gamble; Washington Jordon; John Gately; Thomas and James Frear."[36]

Hall continued his recollection:

They soon began discussing ways and means. Money was to be distributed in the South and a company of horsemen formed, with Ingram as Captain. The company was to be sent to Texas. The money or life of no Union man was to be considered sacred!

For once impulse got the better of me. I cocked my pistol, and pointed it at the leader, thinking how easily I could silence his boastful words, and inwardly, much excited, I scrutinized the band. They were from all climes and conditions, and with all grades of intelligence from the swarthy, low-browed man, with his massive frame, the perfect embodiment of brute force, up to the slender, well-formed and polished gentleman, with his broad, high brow and low, full voice . . .

I lay there for a full minute, with my pistol cocked, hesitating whether to shoot or not; then discretion overcame my valor, for I could not hope to war successfully against such odds, and I attempted to uncock my weapon, but as I did so it went off in the air, and you never saw such a stampede!

Some sprang to their feet and looked wildly around; some crawled on all fours toward the brush; others lay flat on their stomachs in paralyzed fear; but finally all made their way to their horses, which were tied in an opposite direction from where I was.

It was all I could do to keep from laughing at the absurd appearance they presented; but my own case was hazardous, for had but one come in my direction and discovered me this story would probably never have been told or my fate known. But Providence and their own fear protected me.

In half an hour all was still, and I made my way home, but it was this surprise that made them change their place of meeting to the east of San Jose, and not their intention of raiding the town, as the newspapers stated at the time. For sanitary reasons I kept silent about the scare I had given them.

Across the valley and to the east, the new camp's location was near the Arroyo Hondo in Milpitas. It was within two miles of Preston Hodges' ranch. In the transition, Captain Red Fox Ingram abandoned his plan to rob San Jose banks. But it wasn't long before he created a new one: to rob Comstock stagecoaches in El Dorado County.

Captain Ingram decided they needed to scout out potential robbery targets and the lay of the land. Given the right circumstances, Ingram and a small subset of his men would rob a stagecoach. On May 1st, James Grant and James Wilson left for Placerville. Three days later, they met up with Ingram, Baker, and a man named Slade. For two more days, they collected information on stagecoach routes and schedules.

In a town saloon on May 6, Grant got drunk while trying to recruit a local desperado. When Ingram found out, he furiously pulled the plug and ordered everyone out. They fled Placerville and headed a mile north, before the group split in different directions and met up in Stockton.

Once there, Red Fox ordered them back to camp in Santa Clara. He expelled Jim Grant as an untrustworthy maverick. Preston Hodges outfitted Grant with a horse and outfit, and he was booted out of camp.

John A. Robertson, a storekeeper and KGC knight, recruited an employee clerk, Alban Harvey Glasby, to join the group. Glasby had arrived in California the year before from Missouri.

He was about five feet nine inches tall and weighed one hundred and forty pounds. With a light complexion and dark hair without whiskers, he had something of a baby-face look. Some compared him to Billy the Kid.

Robertson gave Glasby a horse, gun, and directions to the Arroyo Hondo camp near Hodges' ranch in early June. At eighteen, Glasby became Captain Ingram's Partisan Rangers' youngest member.

Al Glasby, *Courtesy of John Boessenecker collection*

For James Grant, his Confederate learnings were tenuous. He became a cropper, but that was too tame. He also recruited some partners and freelanced by robbing stages between Salinas and San Jose. He was described in the *Sacramento Union* as *about as thorough a scoundrel as ever stretched hemp.*[37] Don't you just love the language of the times?

James Grant, *Courtesy of John Boessenecker collection*

Ever the ladies' man, Grant awoke one morning after an evening at Katie Kincaid's house to an unpleasant surprise. Undersheriff Hall's Navy Colt revolver barrel was pressed against his nose!

Hall arrested and handcuffed James Grant. Even handcuffed, Grant managed to grab a shotgun and took off. As he ran away, Hall shot him in the back, but Grant survived his wounds. His fate was San Quentin State Prison for robbing the Salinas stage.

As you can clearly see, this wartime crew included some unsavory characters. Hardly the romanticized image of knights operating from castles! Nor did they dignify the term partisan rangers.

But a darker label would soon apply. In a short while, their escapades would transform them from Knights of the Golden Circle and Captain Ingram's Partisan Rangers into something entirely different. They would be forever known as a gang of Placerville stagecoach robbers.

According to several accounts, there was one other leader besides Captain Red Fox Ingram and his Lieutenant, Tom Poole. *Preston Hodges . . . who acted as the group's chaplain and ideologue.*[38]

4
STAGE IS SET

At their Arroyo Hondo camp, Captain Red Fox Ingram gathered his men. He informed them the time was ripe to execute his plan. They needed to ready themselves to rob stagecoaches to finance recruits for the Confederacy.

Jim Wilson opted out after his previous experience in Placerville and decided to remain at camp. Henry Jarboe remained as well. Red Fox had assigned Jarboe an after-the-robbery job. He was to pick up the loot from wherever it would be buried. After waiting until things settled down about a month after the robbery, he would then return to El Dorado County. He would retrieve the buried treasure and deliver it to the Roundtree Brothers in San Francisco. These two brothers, J.O. and Benjamin, were natives of Natchez, Mississippi.

On June 21, 1864, Captain Ingram's Partisan Rangers included Tom Poole, George Baker, John Clendenning, John Creal Bouldware, and Al Glasby. They left the Santa Clara Valley on horseback. The first night, the men stayed in the Livermore Valley at the Mountain House. The next day, they arrived in Stockton and registered at the Pacific Hotel under false names.

Next, they stopped at Jackson and Mokelumne Hill. On June 27, they arrived at the Somerset House north of Fiddletown. Upon arrival, they told the owner, Mrs. Davis, they were traveling to Reese River Valley in Nevada to mine for gold.

Mrs. Davis's housekeeper and friend, Mrs. Maria Reynolds, showed them to their rooms. While Tom Poole and Al Glasby remained, Red Fox took the others down Grizzly Flat Road for target practice. Each man was outfitted with two Navy Colt revolvers.

The next morning, June 28, they left Somerset and staked out the Carson Emigrant Road. Today it's known as the Mormon Emigrant Trail between Highway 88 and Sly Park near Jenkinson Lake. There, they waited in vain for stagecoaches. Apparently, they were either confused or erroneously told the Carson Trail was where the Comstock Washoe stages ran. The actual stagecoach road was located farther north. They needed to be on the Placerville and Carson Valley Road.

When Ingram realized their error, they retreated to Bertram's Hotel. It was also known as the Pacific House or Eighteen Mile House. Today, it's about five miles east of Pollock Pines, just off Highway 50.

The raiders spent a good part of June 29 relaxing there. Red Fox decided to move and checked his rangers into the Six Mile House. They spent the night there. When they awoke the next morning, the stage was truly set to execute their plan.

Early in the morning of June 30, 1864, a group of

passengers milled around the dusty streets of Virginia City, Nevada. Due to high demand fueled by the silver boom, two stagecoaches were soon scheduled to depart. Their destination was the Wells Fargo & Company's Express Office at the Cary House in Placerville. The company located there due to the booming commerce created by Nevada's silver mines.

As the expectant passengers watched, valuable cargo was hoisted onboard the two stagecoaches. The treasure included bags of coins, silver bars, bullion, gold dust, paper, and a strongbox belonging to the Wells Fargo & Company.

During Virginia City's heyday, a normal stagecoach cargo was valued as much as $80,000. In today's currency, that's in the millions. As Wells Fargo Bank retired historian, Dr. Robert J. Chandler, recently disclosed,[39] the stagecoach cargo pattern was considered "up and down."

What that meant was that cargo going "down" from Virginia City to San Francisco transported mostly silver. The stagecoach cargo going "up" from San Francisco to Virginia City transported primarily gold coins. That made the "up" cargo considerably more valuable.

The robbers planned to hold up a "down" stagecoach. But no one knew precisely how much this cargo was worth. Not the drivers, the Wells Fargo employees, nor the passengers.

Anticipating the twelve-hour ride, the passengers mentally prepared for what was ahead. They probably had a good idea of what they were in for from other travelers' stories. Or they might have read advice like these "Tips for Stagecoach Travelers."[40]

> *The best seat inside a stage is the one next to the driver. Even if you have a tendency to sea-sickness when riding backwards — you'll get over it and will get less jolts and jostling . . . Don't growl at the food received at the station — stage companies generally provide the best they can get . . . Don't smoke a*

strong pipe inside the coach. Spit on the leeward side. If you have anything to drink in a bottle pass it around . . . Don't lean or lop over neighbors when sleeping . . . Don't point out where murders have been committed, especially if there are women passengers . . . Don't lag at the wash basin . . . Don't grease your hair, because travel is dusty . . . Don't imagine for a moment that you are going on a picnic . . . Expect annoyances, discomfort, and some hardships.

As was typical, seven passengers crowded inside each stagecoach. Each passenger sat shoulder-to-shoulder with only fifteen inches of sitting space. By comparison, a typical chair width today is eighteen and a half inches!

If that wasn't enough, seven more people climbed on top including one driver and usually two company employees. As they clambered aboard, imagine how each of the two Louis McLane Pioneer Stage Company coaches sagged into the dirt.

Twenty-eight passengers, drivers, and employees braced for the journey ahead. The two passenger trains, as they were

Wells, Fargo & Co's Express Office, C street, Virginia City c1866[41]
Courtesy of Society of California Pioneers

called back then, were scheduled to follow the twisty curvy "highway" only a few minutes apart.

Ned Blair
Courtesy of George Yamamoto collection[42]

In the first bullion-loaded Concord coach, driver Ned Blair readied himself on Virginia City's main street. Blair knew the route well and what was ahead.

During the gold rush, Ned Blair's pioneer family immigrated to El Dorado County from Scotland. His family owned a lumber mill near Sportsman's Hall, the last scheduled stop before Placerville.

Much of the route followed the old pioneer emigrant trail established during gold rush days. The Pony Express trail was abandoned just the year before.

Although Blair had traveled the road many times before, each trip required skill and concentration. The road featured many twists and turns, plus challenging and treacherous descents along steep, narrow canyons. Yes, he was most mindful about the road ahead.

Ned Blair most surely shouted *heeyaaah* at his team of

six horses to start them on the way. A few minutes later, the second bullion-loaded coach followed.

Charley Watson
Courtesy of El Dorado County Historical Museum[43]

Coach two's driver, Charley Watson was equally skilled. He regularly drove the Genoa to Placerville route and knew the area well. In fact, he dreamed of owning a stagecoach stop on the way to Placerville.

Ned Blair and Charley Watson coaxed their teams up the mountainous curves of the Sierra Nevada mountain range's eastern slope. For everyone on board, it was anything but a smooth ride.

The two coaches kicked up clouds of dust as they raced along the trails. The dust cloud barely dissipated behind the first coach before the second coach caught up with the previous dust cloud and kicked up its own.

STAGE IS SET

Courtesy of El Dorado County Historical Museum (04915)[44]

AS THE TWO COACHES LURCHED DOWN THE ROAD,
NO ONE ANTICIPATED JUST HOW EVENTFUL THIS
TRIP WOULD BE.

After Carson Pass, they carefully descended through the valley. Then came the most challenging part. The long, narrow winding road between Lake Bigler (named for the governor and later renamed Tahoe from its original Native American name) and Placerville required skill, knowledge, experience, and even luck. But at times, the twists and turns of the western slope might even have seemed fun.

On average every eight to twelve miles, the drivers halted the teams and passengers at pre-determined stops for well-needed and deserved breaks. From Virgina City, the scheduled stops were: Carson, Glenbrook, Lake Bigler, Yank's, Strawberry Station, Webster's, River-Side Station, Sportsman's

Hall, and then Placerville. Passengers could then travel by railroad to Latrobe, Folsom, and Sacramento.

About ten miles down the western slope from the summit, Ned Blair and Charley Watson pulled their coaches into Strawberry Station. This "refueling" stop for dinner and to change horses was Charley's special place. A year later in 1865, he realized his dream and took over as the lodge's owner-proprietor.

As twilight began, both drivers affixed coach lights before leaving. As they continued along the old Pony Express trail, a very steep drop-off to the south fork of the American River canyon was off to the right. On the left was a steep mountainside screened with ponderosa pines and towering incense cedars.

As dusk settled in, the warm summer evening breezes began turning cool. The front-facing drivers and passengers watched the sun setting in the west directly ahead. It was a week after the summer solstice, the longest day of the year.

Thankfully, it had been a relatively uneventful trip on this final day of June. At least so far. Both drivers felt they should easily make it to Placerville on schedule by midnight.

BUT NO ONE WAS AWARE OF EXACTLY WHAT WAS AHEAD. NOT THE DRIVERS, THE PASSENGERS, NOR THE GANG OF ROBBERS WAITING EXPECTANTLY.

5

BULLION BEND

Sometime between nine and ten p.m., Ned Blair's coach was on the north side of Union Hill just around a bend of Placerville Road. With two distinct bends, he made a sharp turn to the left and then let his team run a mile before making another sharp turn to the right.

After that last curve, it was a straight shot to their destination, the Cary House in Placerville, slightly less than fourteen miles distant. His coach was about two and a half miles before the last stop at Sportsman's Hall.

As Blair negotiated that last major blind curve, he slowed his team to a walk. Around the curve lurked trouble and danger. This place was about to be renamed forever as . . . Bullion Bend.[45]

During the day, this road was heavily traveled. Emigrant wagons and Pioneer stagecoaches shared the road. Imagine what types of traffic jams were created on this narrow road framed by mountains and ravines.

Bullion Bend on Lake Tahoe Wagon Road Map, 1895 (ID 58)
Courtesy of California State Archives, Sacramento

Emigrant Train, Strawberry Valley (17120)
Courtesy of El Dorado County Historical Museum

But at night, the road was only traveled by Pioneer coaches. As Captain Red Fox Ingram waited with his men, he heard the coaches approaching. He whispered to his men, *Keep cool. If they resist, empty all your shots.*⁴⁶

Stagecoach One Stopped

Up ahead, Ned Blair saw a lone figure in the road motioning him to stop. It was hard to see clearly at dusk. Captain Red Fox Ingram emerged from the bushes with a shotgun. He hollered, *Hold on, or I'll fire.*⁴⁷

Tom Poole ran to the lead horse and grabbed the bridle to steady the team. Suddenly, a stagecoach robbers' gang blocked Blair's path.

As Blair sat motionless, Red Fox ordered, *Throw down the strong box.* Blair lied, *I don't have one.* The captain replied, *Then throw down the treasure.* Blair retorted, *Come and get it.*⁴⁸

What guts and nerve! Nonetheless, two robbers climbed up and threw down four sacks of bullion.

Just then, Red Fox heard another approaching coach. He signaled Blair to pull up on the side of the road. He must have thought he just hit the Mother Lode — an unexpected two-for-one jackpot!

Stagecoach Two Stopped

When Charley Watson driving coach two saw the first coach stopped ahead, he pulled up. He handed the passenger next to him his reins and stepped down. He thought they had an accident or some mechanical problem. When he got to within twelve feet of the first coach, a man pointed a gun at him and said, *Hold on, or I'll put a hole through you.*⁴⁹ It was Captain Red Fox Ingram.

Watson backpedaled and resumed his coach seat. While young Al Glasby covered him, Red Fox returned to coach one.

Two robbers covered driver Blair with their sidearms, while

two others secured bags of silver bars. Blair asked them not to rob the passengers. Red Fox replied that he commanded a company of Confederate soldiers. They were Southern gentlemen. He had no such intention to rob or hurt the passengers. They just wanted the Wells, Fargo & Company treasure to recruit more soldiers for the Confederacy.

When Red Fox was satisfied they collected all the treasure, he waived driver Blair to go on. As the coach started off, passenger McDougall, a Virginia City police officer, pointed his pistol out the coach window and shot at Tom Poole. The first shot went wild, but the second one knocked the pistol right out of Poole's hand.

As the first coach quickly disappeared around the bend, the robbers lost any chance to fire back. But they immediately turned and riveted their attention on the second coach eighty feet away stopped just up the road. The robbers were furious. One shouted, *Let's kill every last son-of-a-bitch of them!* [50]

Driver Watson later recalled, *They seemed excited . . . I had to talk good to them to get along with them.*[51] *I said they shouldn't take it out on folks that had nothing to do with what went on. That wasn't fair.*[52]

Watson ordered his passengers not to resist or use their guns, so no one would get shot. But he was equally concerned about preventing his jittery team of horses already spooked from the previous gunfire. They all faced the real danger of tumbling down the steep cliff and canyon side and being dashed to pieces.

Captain Red Fox Ingram also steadied the gang members. As he stroked his long, dyed black whiskers, Ingram restated what he told the first coach driver and passengers. He explained, *Gentlemen, I will tell you who we are. We are not robbers, but a company of Confederate Soldiers. Don't act foolish. We don't want anything of the passengers. All we want* is Wells, Fargo & Co.'s treasure, to assist us to recruit for the Confederate army.[53]

CURIOUS TEENAGER

Unexpectedly, a teenage girl passenger piped up and peppered the captain and gang members with questions. She seemed to sweet-talk and flirt with the robbers.[54]

Are you soldiers? Where are your uniforms? Do you have a flag? I'd like to see it. The captain replied, *We're a little busy right now.* Red Fox then passed a hat asking passengers for donations to their cause. The teenager joked, *I only have a five-cent postage stamp in my pocket. You'll have to take it from me, but I won't give it up without a fight!* When the youngest good-looking robber, Al Glasby, accidently grazed her face with his pistol barrel she exclaimed, *Be careful with that. It might just go off!* An immediate apology followed.

But no one donated to the Confederate cause.

The gang carried on with the business of robbing the stage. They demanded for Charley Watson to throw down the bullion. He replied he had to hold onto the reins. Red Fox directed him to pass the reins to the man sitting on his right. One bandit was told to steady the horses. With four pistols and a shotgun trained on Watson, Red Fox repeated his demand to throw down the bullion. Charley threw down three bags weighing about 250 pounds. Charley's estimate of its value — $20,000.[55]

But that wasn't all the treasure. The robbers asked Watson for the Wells Fargo & Company strong box. Charley said he didn't have one. The man with black whiskers didn't believe him. Red Fox Ingram stepped up, reached over Watson, and pulled the box out of the boot.

Charley said, *Don't take it, there's nothing much but personal stuff from Genoa, in Nevada.* Red Fox replied, *If that is sure enough true, I'll just leave the box by the side of the road where you can get it the next day.*[56]

Watson later recounted the strongbox was worth about $26,000 and contained $2,000 in gold coin and dust.[57] As the gang finished collecting the loot, Captain Red Fox handed a receipt[58] to Charley Watson!

> June ___ 1864
> This to Certify that I have received from Wells Fargo & Co the sum of ___ $ cash ___ for the purpose of outfitting recruits enlisted in California for the Confederate States army
> R Henry Ingram
> Captain Commanding Company C.S.A.

Peo. vs. Poole/Hodges, Trial Transcript, image[59]
Courtesy of California State Archives, Sacramento

Is that crazy or what?

As a final parting command, Red Fox warned Watson that any shots from the coach would invoke return fire in double. He then released them to go on their way.

When Blair's coach reached Sportsman's Hall first, an overlooked detail in the robbers' plan surfaced — the new telegraph line. The alarm was sounded by wire. Word of the double stagecoach robbery flashed over Colonel Bee's grapevine to their destination in Placerville.

There, Sheriff Rogers hastily assembled a posse. Constable George C. Ranney, a deputy sheriff, was awakened out of a deep sleep at his house and headed into the courthouse. Others recruited included Deputies Joseph Staples and John Dick Van Eaton, policemen J.G. Bailey and J.Y. Williamson, a few Pioneer Stage Company employees, and some civilians.

When the second coach pulled in to town, Rogers added coach driver Charley Watson to his posse for a total of thirteen men. Undersheriff Jim Hume was away on official business.

Curious Teenager Explains

Before heading off with the posse, Charley quizzed the teenager why she chatted and maybe even flirted with the gang members. She replied, *It was dark. I wanted to be able to identify them later through their voices.*

Another passenger commented, *She was smarter than we men were . . . and I might add, considerably more self-possessed. She exhibited the grit of the right kidney . . . and considerable cuteness as well as bravery. If I knew her name I would give it to Chief Burke with a recommendation that she be employed on detective duty.*[60] Chief Martin T. Burke was police chief in San Francisco. Unfortunately, this savvy teenager's name was never recorded. So far, her identity is lost to history.

The posse saddled up between 2:30 and 3:00 a.m. and galloped off in search of the robbers. Sheriff Rogers split the posse into two groups. His group included driver Charley Watson and headed to the crime scene.

The other group of three men traveled southeast on a shortcut from Bullion Bend towards the Placerville-Diamond Springs Road. They crossed the North Fork of the Cosumnes River hoping to find the robbers' tracks.

Deputies George C. Ranney, John Van Eaton, and Joe Staples traveled south down Sly Park Road and east along Pleasant Valley Road. They squinted in the dark and found tracks of *four, five, maybe six tracks heading south.*[61]

Ranney figured they found the bandits' trail. He sent deputy Van Eaton, who had the fastest horse, to alert Sheriff

Rogers and get reinforcements. Then Ranney and Staples followed the gang's trail along Mt. Aukum Road.

As the sun's rays peeked over the treetops and mountains, Ranney and Staples could see the outline of a two-story house ahead through the early morning dawning light. Sunrise was almost upon them.

6

LONG ARM OF THE LAW

When deputies George Ranney and Joe Staples rode up to the Somerset House, Ranney immediately noticed a shotgun leaning up against an outside wall. He found the housekeeper, Maria Reynolds, and asked her about visitors. She indicated there were six men inside an upstairs bedroom.

Ranney realized they were most surely the robbers. In a brazen or even foolhardy display of courage, Ranney walked right inside and startled four disheveled men. They had arrived only an hour and a half before.[62] Awakened from their slumber, the desperadoes grasped their holsters ready to draw.

As Ranney sized up the situation, he calmly greeted them with a friendly, *Good morning. Have you seen or heard anyone pass by here in the night?* What bravado! Red Fox replied, *No*.[63]

Ranney turned and exited through the same door, then retreated down the steps. Staples met him on the porch sporting the shotgun already cocked. Ranney placed his hand lightly but squarely on Staples' shoulder and whispered, *Don't go in. We're right upon them.*[64]

Ranney felt Staples' muscles tighten and recalled an incident. In a recent pursuit, Deputy Staples missed apprehending the Ike McCallum band of outlaws. When Deputy Van Eaton was wounded by gunfire, Staples' spooked horse ran off with him astride.

In a barroom after the episode, he overheard a patron say, *Staples took damned good care to keep out of danger.* Staples angrily replied, *The next time I go I'll be brought back dead or I'll bring back my man!*[65] That turned out to be prophetic.

Staples pushed right by Ranney who had no choice but to follow right behind him. Staples burst through the door and shouted, *You're my prisoners. Surrender!*[66] He trained his shotgun on one robber, then another. They both reached to draw. After ten to fifteen seconds of tense standoff with Staples shifting his aim from robber to robber, a hail of bullets greeted Staples.

He squeezed off one round and then a second just as two shots pierced him. One hit him square in the chest. Both bullets traveled cleanly through his body which created four holes. Staples fell dead on the floor at Ranney's feet, while a blast from Staples' shotgun hit Tom Poole squarely on the side of his face knocking him onto the bed.

Deputy Ranney could count — the odds were dramatically against him. He backed down the platform, fired twice, and hightailed it out of there — dodging bullets while trying to find cover. Shots rained at him from what seemed to be all sides. A bullet struck his side and lodged in his lower back. But he kept running.

Ranney found cover behind the horses, but the gang discovered him. He sprang up and ran towards a large boulder about a hundred and fifty feet away. Shots were coming at him from all angles. As he continued running, he turned sideways to shoot back at his pursuers.

Suddenly, another bullet struck Ranney's right side just below his heart. He coughed up blood, crumpled on the ground, and raised his hands moaning, *Hold on. I am an officer. Don't fire any more. You men have killed me.*[67]

As five bandits rushed in with pointed guns, they demanded, *Is there any more of you fellows around here?* Weakly Ranney said, *No.* One yelled, *How in the hell did you find us so soon?* Another taunted him, *Did you think that two damned Yankees could capture six Confederate soldiers?*[68]

Ranney, badly wounded, was now surrounded. The captain mused, *Do you suppose that a Confederate officer's going to surrender to a damn Yankee? We are Missouri Bush Whackers. All of us.*[69]

They quickly sized up Ranney as no further threat and backed off. They decided not to finish him off yet. As they half drug him back towards the inn, George Baker put a gun to Ranney's head and taunted him: *God Damn you. I will blow your brains out. You have killed poor Pool (sic).*[70]

Al Glasby hollered at Baker, *Hold on. Stop. You can't do that. The man who shot Pool (sic) is already dead.*[71] He meant Staples.

When they reached the inn's porch, Ranney collapsed in an old chair. He was bleeding at the mouth. Just then, housekeeper Maria Reynolds burst onto the scene. She shoved aside two bandits and cried out, *Ain't you ashamed? Shooting a dead man!*[72] An old man, probably a neighbor attracted by the commotion, echoed Maria: *Don't shoot or kill a man who is dyin' already!*[73]

Boulware took full advantage of the situation and stole Ranney's money and guns. George Baker, with a swift kick, rolled over Staples' corpse. He said, *That's one less Union officer.* He took Staples' pistol, watch, and three $20 gold pieces.[74]

Inside, Tom Poole lay wounded on the bed. Glasby was sent inside to grab Poole's money and both guns. Glasby brought them outside. Poole staggered out the front door. His comrades-in-crime told him they were leaving. Poole pleaded to be taken with them. They said no but promised to send a buggy to take him to Fiddletown. Again, Poole said he'd go, if they got his horse. They said no . . . again. They added if any lawmen came looking for them, he was to crawl in the bushes and hide.[75]

The gang members mounted the deputies' now stolen horses — and left their weaker ones behind. They fled this chaotic scene of mayhem — leaving two lawmen, one dead and one dying, plus a wounded comrade in their dust. Essentially, Poole was left to die or take the rap as the fall guy.

Meanwhile, Maria Reynolds attended to the seriously wounded Ranney. With help from the landlady, Mrs. Davis, they managed to get him inside the house and placed him on an old mattress.

As the women worked on him, Ranney's blood flowed across the room and pooled on the floorboards. Ranney cried out, *Pull my shirt open and see if you can do something to stop this bleeding, or in the next faint I'll go off.*[76] They managed to tear it open and saw the flow of blood decreasing. They saw signs of his blood clotting.

Everyone at Somerset House wondered what happened to the posse with reinforcements. When the posse arrived at Sportsman's Hall, driver Ned Blair mistakenly identified Thomas Finney and William Becher as members of the gang. Sheriff Rogers took them into custody and grilled them mercilessly. When Deputy Van Eaton brought news of the bandits' trail leading towards Somerset House, Rogers was convinced he had two of them already arrested and continued his interrogation. Van Eaton finally convinced him the real robbers were probably at the Somerset House. Undersheriff James B. Hume, who missed the action due to official business out of the county, arrived and joined the posse.

But it was noon before they arrived at the shootout scene — giving the robbers six hours of daylight between them and the posse. Hume was a great friend of Staples. When he saw his dead body, he was overcome with grief and rage.

Under-sheriff James B. Hume c 1872 (04521.1)
Courtesy of El Dorado County Historical Museum

Good Doctor Arrives

Just in the nick of time, a Diamond Springs' physician on his way to Grizzly Flats dismounted and entered the room. After a quick examination of Ranney, Doctor H.W.A. Worthen, pronounced gravely, *Looks pretty bad for you, Mister. There's two bullets in here. I can't do much for you, but I'll do what I can.*[77]

Fortunately, what the physician saw as two bullet wounds was only one bullet that struck on the right side and came out at the opposite breast. It left a clean hole. Dr. Worthen saved Ranney's life.

While Dr. Worthen cared for Ranney, Sheriff Rogers placed Tom Poole in custody. Of course, Poole denied any robbery involvement. He told Rogers he was the former Monterey County Sheriff. He claimed to meet the others just that very morning.

After the good doctor treated Poole's injuries, Sheriff Rogers placed Tom Poole under arrest. When Hume realized the wounded and still very much alive prisoner was probably his friend's killer, it made him furious. But he kept his cool and mapped out the crime scene in the bedroom. He wanted to be able to diagram it later for a trial. But he also felt frantic to track down the gang. He wanted to get in on the chase.

Finally, they wrapped up their work. Staples' corpse was retrieved and loaded in a wagon. It must have been a long heart-wrenching ride back to Placerville late on July 1.

Somerset House, scene of the shootout. (05135)
Courtesy of the El Dorado County Historical Museum

Joseph M. Staples' Funeral

The next day, July 2, was a sad occasion. Staples was well-liked. His close friend, Deputy Van Eaton, donated his own gravesite to bury Staples in the Placerville Union Cemetery. Staples was mourned and memorialized on this day. His funeral notice[78] with obituary describes the extraordinary event.

> FUNERAL OF JOSEPH M. STAPLES.—Joseph M. Staples, who was killed by the stage robbers at the Somerset House while attempting to arrest them on Friday of last week, was buried by Neptune Engine Co. No. 2, of this city, of which he was a member, on Saturday afternoon. His body was brought to this city on Friday night, and placed in the hall of the company's building, which had been shrouded in mourning.— Rev. Mr. Peirce, on Saturday afternoon, preached a feeling and impressive funeral sermon, which was listened to by members of the Fire Department, county officials, a large number of ladies and other friends of the deceased. He also read a beautiful and affectionate letter, breathing the very essence of purity and piety, from the aged mother of the deceased to her loved son, which he had received but a day or two before his tragical death, and which was found on his body. His funeral was largely attended by the citizens of Placerville and Coloma—he having been an old and esteemed resident of the latter place. He was an estimable citizen, an excellent officer and a warm friends—brave, true hearted and generous— modest, courteous and educated, and his death is deeply deplored by those who knew him best. He was born in Ireland. His grandfathers, father, and two brother were clergymen.

Staples was the first El Dorado County peace officer killed in the line of duty. It would be more than one hundred and twenty-six years later in 1990, before the next El Dorado County police officer was shot in the line of duty.[79]

Joseph M. Staples' Gravestone
Placerville Union Cemetery[80]

7

CHASE IS ON

Meanwhile, the gang of desperados galloped away from Somerset House. The gang rode south for several miles and then headed off trail. The rough mountainous terrain between the Consumnes and Mokelumne rivers made it easier to hide their tracks from the posse that was surely chasing them.

Sheriff Rogers' posse included Undersheriff Hume and stagecoach driver Charley Watson. They were in hot pursuit of the stagecoach robbers' gang. Off in the distance as Red Fox Ingram rode along the mountain ridge crests, he caught glimpses of horsemen on their trail.

Coincidently, Ike McCallum's gang was hiding out in the same general area. In May after their shootout with Hume, Staples, and Van Eaton, these horse-thieves were keeping a low profile.

When Sheriff Rogers' posse arrived in the area, they flushed out McCallum's gang. The gang made a quick escape towards a new hide-out.

At dusk on July 2, the weary Bullion Bend outlaws selected a hide-out on the mountaintop near Rail Road Flats on the Mokelumne River's South Fork. Camped near the summit, the desperados posted a guard and fell fast asleep. Little did they know they had selected the same hide-out area as McCallum's gang.

About midnight, the Bullion Bend gang's lookout sounded the alarm. The posse was heading their way! While some were ready to take a stand, Red Fox decided this was not the time to fight. He ordered a retreat.

With no time to saddle up their horses, the gang members grabbed their weapons, loot, and supplies. They fled down the mountain's backside. Besides their horses, they even left behind a silver bar from the robbery!

As fate would have it, the lookout was mistaken. The horsemen he spotted were not the posse. They were Ike McCallum's gang.

Now horse-less, the Bullion Bend outlaws were on foot. They . . . *struck out on foot for the Valley, crossing the San Joaquin by ferry and forcing the ferryman to land them downriver from the wharf to avoid detection.*[81]

The posse meanwhile fanned out through the hills and ravines but lost their prey's trail. After seven days, they called a halt to their search. Another posse from Jackson in Amador County relieved them. According to author Richard Dillon, "they were attracted by Wells, Fargo's reward of $500 for each robber convicted — or killed while resisting arrest — plus twenty percent of any treasure recovered."[82]

CHASE IS ON

> PROMISES OF REWARDS CIRCULATED THROUGHOUT
> THE MOTHER LODE. EVEN MORE ENTICING—
> THE RUMORS OF BURIED TREASURE.

The El Dorado County posse's efforts were praised by the state's press. The *California Police Gazette* commented: *So continued as untiring a pursuit, we venture to say, as has been made in this state. Over mountains and through gulches, these officers pursued their way, night and day, across the roughest portions of the State of California, including Amador, Calaveras, and San Joaquin counties, often without food or rest, until the robbers, being forced to travel on foot, of course, could not be followed. The chase reflects the greatest credit on Sheriff Rogers and all concerned.*[83]

After the posse returned empty-handed, Deputy Sheriff J.D. Van Eaton began formulating a plan.[84] He schemed to take advantage of his South Carolina heritage and upbringing.

Van Eaton checked into jail and posed as another inmate. With his soft southern accent, South Carolina heritage and upbringing, he hoped to gain Poole's confidence with sympathetic statements for the Southern cause.

Another account in the *Biography of James B. Hume* by Richard Dillon,[85] gives the credit to Undersheriff Hume. Either way and regardless of who implemented it, this strategy was brilliant. It might even have been a collaborative effort by two police officer colleagues.

Think about it for a moment. Abandoned by his rangers or crime cohorts depending on your perspective, Poole was very intelligent. He was locked in jail. Staples was dead. He could see the proverbial "handwriting on the wall." Promises and expectations of POW treatment never materialized.

In El Dorado County, no one saw Poole's actions stemming from a military operation engagement. Plus, in the Wild West of yesteryear, legal "Miranda rights" were not a consideration. Before long, he spilled the beans and named names.

Poole implicated his fellow gang members and freely gave his inquisitors information on each one. He also revealed the location of the buried treasure. After all, did he owe any more to the cause or his comrades? They deserted him to take the rap!

Meanwhile, the Bullion Bend outlaws trekked on foot two hundred plus miles. A week later, they arrived at their destination: Preston Hodges' ranch in Santa Clara County. They needed to report what happened.

BACK AT THE RANCH

On about July 9, the gang started arriving back at the ranch, and the reports started. Al Glasby was the second robber to arrive. Bouldware was already there. Ingram and Baker came later.

Over breakfast, Glasby gave Hodges his report.[86] When Hodges heard what happened to the treasure, he apparently remarked, *I'm sorry you didn't get away with all the bullion.* When Glasby said the men lost their horses, Hodges replied, *That's just as well. If you had brought them back, they might connect them to me.*

Hodges went into San Jose and bought provisions for Glasby and Bouldware. Upon his return, Hodges suggested to Glasby and Ingram they had better hide out at the Santa Cruz mountain camp above Saratoga. He knew lawmen were spying on his ranch. He was afraid to be seen with these two men any longer.

Glasby later recounted the continued conversation. *Bulware (sic) says he's goin' back to Somerset House in a month to get the bullion bar we hid there before we left. Hodges says in a month there should be no danger, but Bulware (sic) should stay there, an' Hodges would send someone to get up there to get the bar at*

Somerset an' the other one we left at Rail Road Flat if it's still there.[87]

The gang wasted no time sitting around and thinking about "what ifs." They immediately planned another robbery. This time, the target was either the New Almaden Quicksilver Mine or its large payroll transported by evening stagecoach on July 15.

On July 14 as author John Boessenecker recounts, *Ingram, Baker, Clendenning, Bouldware, and Glasby showed up at the ranch house of Edward Hill, on the Almaden road, a mile and a half from town.*[88] They used a cover story of expected friends passing by this road and wanted to stay the night. Hill put them up in an empty building.

The following day, rancher Hill became suspicious as the group hung around. After some careless comments about a planned robbery, Hill slipped away. He told his neighbor, Colonel Kendrick, to get word to Santa Clara County Sheriff John Hicks Adams — convinced this was a dangerous gang.

Sheriff John Hicks Adams
Courtesy, History San Jose

Sheriff Adams quickly assembled a posse. Members included Deputy Sheriffs J.M. Brownlee, G.W. Reynolds, Fred Morris, City Marshal J. C. Potter, Constable Robert Scott, A. Bowman, and three other citizens.[89] Their surnames were Senter, Gould, and Willis.

The posse headed off at six o'clock and surrounded the gang's temporary residence, a small whitewashed house. It was at sunset on the 15th — the evening the large payroll was due by stagecoach.

With his men ready, Sheriff Adams shouted, *Come out and deliver yourselves up!* Instead, the gang rushed out firing. Each had two pistols blazing away. Brownlee's leg was struck by two bullets. A bullet struck Sheriff Adams but was deflected by his vest's pocket watch.

In a hail of shots, robber John C. Bouldware was gunned down and died on the spot. A second robber, John Clendenning, ran towards cover. His back was riddled with buckshot from Sheriff Adams' shotgun, but he leapt a fence and fled into the chaparral. A third robber, Al Glasby, unloaded his guns while running backward from the posse.

Glasby's first gun ran out of bullets. His second gun jammed when its butt was shot off. Knowing he was hopelessly outgunned, he surrendered. Glasby had obediently followed Captain Ingram's earlier orders exactly as instructed at Bullion Bend — *to empty all your shots.* Red Fox would have been proud of his young ranger.

Afterwards, Glasby's captors discovered his overcoat pierced with seven bullet holes. But amazingly, he was not wounded. More than forty shots were fired in the gun battle.

During the shootout's chaos, some believe Red Fox and George Baker escaped. Others believe they were never present. Author J.G. Kearney says eyewitness accounts never mentioned the presence of Ingram and Baker. Whether or not the two ringleaders were there, the Bullion Bend robbers' escapades now approached legendary status. What is known — Ingram and Baker disappeared. Their whereabouts remain an unsolved mystery. But other dramatic scenes were still ahead.

Sheriff Adams' posse brought in Bouldware's corpse with Glasby in tow. As the eighteen-year-old was thrown in San Jose's jail, Glasby knew his "jig was up." Not surprisingly, his captors did not consider him a prisoner of war.

A fresh search party later found Clendenning at one in the morning and arrested him. When brought in, he lived just long enough to confess by spilling his guts on what he knew about the gang. He died at ten o'clock.

Hoping to gain his captors' favor, Al Glasby squealed and identified the rest of the gang. One newspaper reported, *Young Glasby, who was recently arrested near San Jose and taken to Placerville, having been on the ground when both the robbery and murder took place, made a full statement before the Grand Jury of the origin, objects and operations of the gang of robbers and on his testimony the parties now arrested were indicted.*[90]

Glasby's testimony before the Grand Jury implicated others and quickened the legal pace. Added to Poole's confession combined with the Somerset House eyewitnesses, the El Dorado County judge, Samuel W. Brockway, had more than enough grounds to issue arrest warrants. The individuals named were:

RUFUS H. INGRAHAM	JAMES GRANT
GEORGE H. BAKER	____ WARD
ALBAN H. GLASBY	____ MARSHALL
THOMAS J. WATKINS	JOE GAMBLE ^ GATELY
HENRY JARBOE	JOHN INGRAHAM
GEORGE CROSS	____ JORDAN
JOHN A. ROBINSON	____ HODGES
WALLACE CLENDENING	THOMAS FREAR
JAMES WILSON	JOHN FREAR

Typical of this era's documents, some names were inaccurate. Handwriting and educational levels varied. Memory lapses or misinterpretations were common.

Poole later claimed the captain's real name was Ralph Henry rather than Rufus H. Other Red Fox surname variants included Ingrim, Ingren, and Ingram. The later surname appears to be most accurate.

Alban Glasby was sometimes called Al Gillespie. John A. Robinson's last name was truly Robertson and properly identified later. Wallace Clendenning's brother, John, was missing on the list. John C. Bouldware was occasionally Bulwer or Bulware, and he used the alias John Creel. He also wasn't listed in the group of initial warrants.

John Ingraham's name was also given as Ingren or Ingram. It's believed he was a close relative of the Red Fox — possibly a brother, nephew, or cousin. The indictment tied Joe Gamble's name to Gatley. But Gatley was a separate individual whose first name was John.

The warrants did not list first names for Ward, Marshall, Jordan, and Hodges. As the legal system proceeded, most of the names were sorted out and properly changed for the record. Even Poole's surname, in most court documents, is usually listed as Pool without the "e."

On July 29 with arrest warrants in hand, Sheriff Rogers sent Undersheriff Hume and Deputy Van Eaton on a mission. They left immediately and headed towards the hotbed of Copperhead activity: Santa Clara County.

Armed not only with the arrest warrants, they planned to enlist help and gain extra firepower. The same day, Sheriff John Hicks Adams and his posse greeted them. Newspaper columnist Richard Hughey recounted the scene: *A band was playing and four infantry companies of the local militia were summoned and were standing by ready for any secessionist uprising.*[91]

Three men had already been killed and four wounded — two seriously.

Governor Low's Reward Issued

Meanwhile in Sacramento on August 2, Governor Low signed a $500 reward for each robber's arrest. As is typical in government work, the political wheels turned slowly. The reward was issued on August 4.

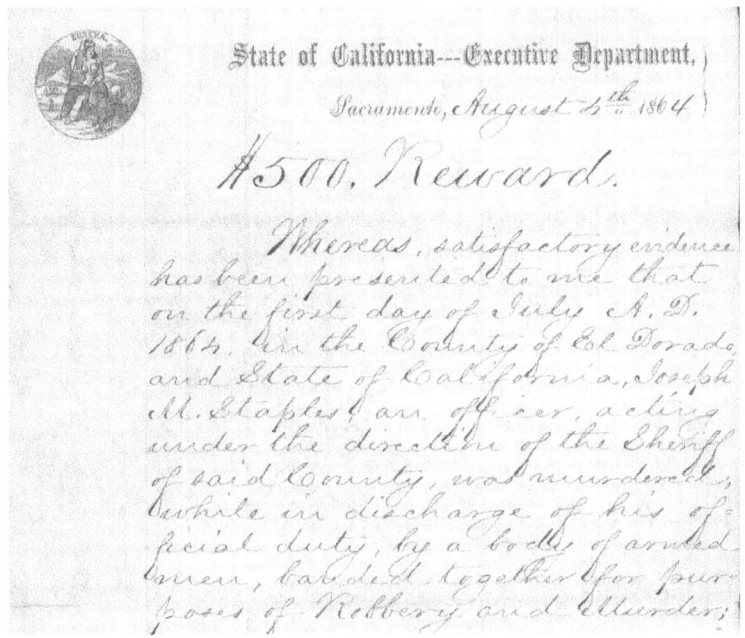

Governor's Offer of Reward, Aug. 4, 1864, (F3671:122)
Courtesy of the California State Archives, Secretary of State, Sacramento

At least two reward copies of this are known to exist. One is in the California State Archives and another in the El Dorado County Museum archives. Right after the holdup, Wells Fargo posted a similar $500 reward notice for each Bullion Bend robber caught dead or alive.

Arrests

On August 4, the combined forces of Deputy Van Eaton and Undersheriff James B. Hume, Sheriff John Adams, his deputies and posse, plus backed by four companies of infantry, in two teams interrupted Copperhead meetings in Santa Clara County. They arrested ten men implicated in the robbery: Henry Jarboe, George Cross, J. A. Robertson, Wallace Clendenning, Joseph Gamble, John Ingram, H. Gatley, Thomas Frear, John Frear, and Preston Hodges.

The prisoners were transported to join Tom Poole and Al Glasby, already in custody in Placerville. The report in a Sacramento newspaper described a memorable scene.[92]

> **The El Dorado Stage Robbers**. – *Deputy Sheriffs Hume and Van Eaton, of El Dorado county, arrived in the city yesterday morning by the San Francisco steamer, with ten prisoners arrested in Santa Clara county. They had been indicted by the Grand Jury of El Dorado as accessories to the robbery of Wells, Fargo & Co's Express near Placerville, . . . and the murder which followed in the same connection by the killing of Deputy Sheriff Staples at the Somerset House . . .*
>
> *They were brought up on the boat handcuffed in couples. On arriving at the levee they were placed in an omnibus and taken to the station house. After breakfasting they were taken to the depot of the Sacramento Valley Railroad Company, and at half-past six o'clock left for Placerville.*
>
> *At Folsom a volunteer guard of nearly one hundred mounted men, from Placerville, were in waiting, and escorted the officers and prisoners the remainder of the journey home. The attendance of this guard was deemed necessary on account of rumors having got afloat that an attempt would be made to rescue the prisoners. As one brave and efficient officer of the county, Staples had already been murdered by a portion of*

this gang, the citizens of the county feel determined that the crime shall not be repeated.

Imagine this scene. The balcony of the Cary House overlooks Main Street. It's filled with curious onlookers packed in like sardines. They jostle each other straining to get the best possible viewing position.

Some onlookers might have warmed up for the occasion at the Arch Saloon next door. In fact, that saloon may have been where gang member James Grant got drunk which aborted the initial planned robbery. The crowd's ever-increasing buzz fills the air.

Cary House on Main Street, Placerville (4402)
Courtesy of the El Dorado County Historical Museum

Along with the curious balcony onlookers, the entire town packs Main Street. Anxiously, everyone strains to catch the first glimpse of what's coming. They hold their breath and point when they hear and see the oncoming caravan of mounted officers and prisoners. After all, these notorious stagecoach robbers caused the death of their beloved deputy sheriff.

Finally, ten prisoners handcuffed in pairs arrive in two wagons escorted by one hundred mounted men. As they enter Placerville from the west, they pass right by the Cary House just below the balcony. The hotel's lobby houses the Wells, Fargo and Company Express Office. The robbery's stolen loot belonged to them.

The prisoners' caravan, or parade as some would characterize it, continues directly east up Main Street to the county courthouse. The prisoners' destination: building 25 on this map's right just below Union Street.[93]

Placerville Lithograph Map (15866)
Courtesy of El Dorado County Historical Museum

After their courthouse arrival, the prisoners were arraigned. They were formally charged for crimes based on evidence given by fellow conspirators Al Glasby, who turned state's evidence, and Thomas Poole, who confessed.

> **The Stage Robbers.** – *Yesterday, (sic August 19) in the District Court, . . . ten of the persons who were indicted for the murder of Deputy Sheriff Joseph M. Staples, were arraigned, attended by their counsel, Messrs. Hurlburt & Edgerton and*

J.M. Williams. *The Court allowed them until 4 o'clock P.M. today, to plead to the indictment. – Placerville Democrat, 20th August.*[94]

Old County Courthouse, Placerville (04957)
Courtesy of El Dorado County Historical Museum

From Main Street, the jail was to the left of and adjacent to the courthouse. A ten-foot high fence ran perpendicular and behind the jail. It framed the jail yard, where gallows were built and convicted felons hung.

After their arraignment, the prisoners were led by the stairway from the annex's porch through the jail yard used for public hangings. Did they glance around and imagine their fate?

The basement was entirely devoted to the jail. It adjoined a room reserved for insane cases. All basement rooms opened into the jail yard, which was enclosed on the west and north by the high board fence. The new arrivals joined Tom Poole, whose wound healed during his time in jail, and Al Glasby who ratted on them.

Imagine the thoughts and conversations. As Poole peered out from his jail cell bars, what was he thinking? The gang members who abandoned Poole at the Somerset House shootout, what were they thinking? Did they say anything to each other? Were they glad to see their comrades-in-arms? What did young Al Glasby say? Did he just listen and watch?

IF JAIL CELLS COULD TALK, WE MIGHT NEED TO CLOSE OUR EARS!

Locked up in his cell, what was going through Preston Hodges' mind? He believed he supported a legitimate military operation. If it ever came to it, he believed he would be treated as a prisoner-of-war. But that's not how it was viewed in El Dorado County's seat — Placerville. After all, it was formerly known as Hangtown.

Right away, legal wrangling occurred. Thomas Frear and John Frear were released. The defense attorneys filed for a change of venue. Their contention was simple. An unbiased trial was impossible in El Dorado County.

Defense counsel requested to move the trial to Santa Clara County. Instead, Judge Samuel W. Brockway granted a venue change to Sacramento County for all the prisoners with two exceptions. The purported leaders of the gang, Tom Poole and Preston Hodges, were to stand trial for murder in Placerville. The courthouse clock was ticking.

El Dorado County Courthouse, Original Courtroom Clock
Courtesy of Bill Cole collection

8
TRIALS

Tom Poole's trial was first on the docket. On August 26, the packed courtroom crowd eagerly anticipated the testimony's start. Scores of people outside clambered to get seats inside.

Several newspaper reporters witnessed the events from the front row. They represented the *San Francisco Alta California*, the *Sacramento Union*, the *San Francisco Bulletin*, and the *San Jose Mercury*. Many other newspapers filed their reports for their distant readers. The *Sacramento Union* reporter labeled the trial *one of the most important and interesting criminal cases ever tried in the state.*[95]

Poole's attorney team was disadvantaged from the start of his trial. Two attorneys were from Alpine County, Carl Edgerton and S. Hurlburt. One came from Santa Clara County,

James W. Williams. They were all on "foreign turf." No "home court advantage" here.

The jury was chosen from a panel of forty-five El Dorado County residents. The jury's twelve men selected were: *G.W. Parsons, S.P. Knight, H.C. Murgotten, R.H. Fergusson, W.C. Ridenour, A. Bernie, S. Roberts, Samuel Black, A. Van Vleck, Charles Hart, C.L. Crisman, and J.W. McCall.*[96]

As newspaper columnist Richard Hughey noted, "Defense counsel had a particularly difficult time . . . The prosecution's case was solid."[97]

After all, Poole confessed to participating in the robbery. He was found at the murder's crime scene with his face riddled with shotgun pellets. The prosecuting attorneys might have considered this case a "slam dunk." The People's case prosecution team consisted of five attorneys: El Dorado County District Attorney J.J. Williams; James C. Goods and N. Greene Curtis of Sacramento; and James M. McShafter, of San Francisco, who represented Wells, Fargo and Company.

Their witness lineup contained recognizable names. These individuals were directly involved in the robbery's events and aftermath.

GEO C RANNEY	CHAS WATSON
MARIA REYNOLDS	W. H. ROGERS
L. W. RUMSEY	ALBAN H. GLASBY
H.W.A WORTHEN	J D VAN EATON

The prosecution called its first witness — Placerville Constable and Deputy Sheriff George C. Ranney. Ranney testified that on July 1, he was awakened at 1:30 a.m. and told two Pioneer stages were robbed of eight sacks of bullion and some gold coin and dust. He rushed over to the courthouse to help assemble the posse in the morning's wee hours.

Ranney first detailed his role in the posse and tracking the gang. He laid out the events at the Somerset House before and after the shootout. Along with housekeeper Mrs. Maria Reynolds' testimony, the two eyewitnesses provided key details of Deputy Sheriff Joseph M. Staples' death and Ranney's shootout with the gang.

Stagecoach driver Charley Watson's testimony was also crucial to the prosecution's case. Because of the venue change for others arrested, Poole was the only stagecoach robber on trial. Captain Ingram had vanished, and Glasby turned state's evidence and would testify later. In his court testimony, Watson singly identified Tom Poole and placed him at the scene of the robbery.

Watson refuted defense claims it was too dark to identify the robbers. Watson testified he affixed coach running lights at the Strawberry stop prior to the robbery. He added that the running lights illuminated three robbers clearly: Captain Red Fox Ingram, Tom Poole, and Al Glasby.

Sheriff Rogers followed Watson's testimony by detailing the chase after the shootout. Al Glasby testified the gang fired thirteen shots in the bedroom. Red Fox fired eight shots, and Bouldware fired five shots. He also identified Tom Poole's role as, *Captain Ingram's lieutenant. You know, second in command.*[98]

Columnist Richard Hughey offered this insight into the trial's proceedings. He wrote, "Attorney Hurlburt conducted most of the cross-examinations of the People's witnesses. He got particularly frustrated in his attempt to impeach Glasby's credibility. At one point he snarled, *'He's a better answerer than anyone I have ever met before.'* Bang! Down came Judge Brockway's gavel. Hurlburt had been warned earlier against such outburst. This time he was sternly rebuked."[99]

On September 1, the prosecution rested its case. The defense lawyer's motion for Poole's dismissal was denied. Judge

Brockway instructed the jurors they could find the defendant guilty of murder in the first degree, murder in the second degree, or manslaughter. He also gave them instructions. If they believed he was innocent of the charges with reasonable doubt, they could find him not guilty.

Given Poole's jailhouse admission of complicity and the eyewitness testimony, the jury's deliberations were swift. The jurors needed only fifteen minutes to return their verdict: guilty of murder in the first degree.

When the verdict was read in the courtroom, the *Sacramento Union* reporter noted, *The prisoner turned slightly pale and for an instant a sneer flitted across his countenance, then it settled into the same gloomy, morose appearance he had borne during the trial.*[100]

Next up was Preston Hodges.

Preston Hodges' Trial

As Preston Hodges' trial began, one newspaper reporter described him as *a well-dressed, apparently well-to-do man, rather large sized, perhaps forty-five or fifty years old, with a florid face, and flowing and very sandy beard and whiskers. He puts on a look of assured confidence, yet it is evident upon close observation that he is watching all the proceedings with anxious keenness.*[101]

The jammed courtroom expected important disclosures and developments. The case proceeded smoothly. The prosecution's docket listed seventeen witnesses. Several had already testified at Poole's trial. Several witnesses from Santa Clara County established that Hodges' ranch was used for "Secessionist and Copperhead meetings."[102] They were paid $40 in travel expenses.

The prosecution again called several witnesses to testify as to the details of the robbery and shootout. They included driver Charley Watson, Deputy George Ranney, and housekeeper Maria Reynolds among others. Then Al Glasby, one of the gang's robbers, was again called to testify.

The prosecution delved deeply into Glasby's interactions with Hodges.[103] The prosecution attorney started with, *Where did you first meet the defendant?* Glasby replied, *In the foothills east of San Jose.* Question, *At his home?* Answer, *Yes, it's about 15 miles east of San Jose. We went there to prepare for going to rob the stages. We wanted to raise money to recruit men for the Confederate Army.*

Glasby testified his employer, John Robertson, initially asked him if he wanted to join the Southern Army. He said Robertson provided him with a pistol and a horse and gave him directions to attend a meeting at Hodges' house.

But when the next witness was called, it must have brought a collective gasp from the crowd.

TOM POOLE WAS CALLED TO THE WITNESS STAND FOR THE PROSECUTION. REALLY! NO ONE CAN MAKE THIS UP. IT'S ONE HUNDRED PERCENT TRUE. A CONVICTED MURDERER WAS ABOUT TO TESTIFY FOR THE PROSECUTION ATTORNEYS WHO CONVICTED HIM. IMAGINE THE COURTROOM BUZZ!

After Poole was sworn in under oath, he introduced himself: *I am the man tried and convicted of the murder of Deputy Sheriff Joe Staples.*[104] The judge most likely hammered his gavel warning the crowd, *Order in the court. Order in the court!*

Poole admitted he was one of a band of men who met at Hodges' ranch. He identified Ingram as a captain in the Confederate Army. Baker told him he had seen Ingram's commission. They plotted to rob stages in El Dorado County to equip an outfit for the Confederacy. He said his personal conversations with Hodges were about the enterprise's purpose. Poole testified:

Hodges said he did not consider any harm as the northern people were robbing our people back at home and we all expressed the same opinion. It was not proposed that Hodges should go–of course not; he only said he saw no harm in it and in that connection referred to the raids on the southern people. We were determined to raise funds to go South and if we could not go peaceable we intended to raise an insurrection in the state of California. I presume that Hodges knew that. It was talked over at his house and he was in and out; He was a man with a family, but we had no secrets there.[105]

Poole said the gang camped two miles from Hodges' home. He reiterated:

We conversed about the subject of the enterprise frequently at his house. Hodges did nothing more than feed us and furnish provisions while there. He said he considered it no harm to fit out a company here for the South, that it was about the same thing robbing in this country as it was in the South where the Northern people were going down and robbing and murdering; he considered it would be the same thing in this county if we should rob. Hodges joined in these conversations. We all thought there was no harm in robbing the stages or taking any means to fit up a company to go to the South.

When the rangers were ready for their mission, they assembled at Hodges' house on June 21. When they mounted their horses to leave for El Dorado County, Preston Hodges joined them on horseback and led them up the Altamonte Mountain pass. When the riders reached the crest, Hodges pointed the way to El Dorado County. As the gang rode on, Hodges' departing words of encouragement were, *God be with you.*[106]

One would imagine Poole's statement created a gasp and buzz in the courtroom onlookers. But there was more testimony to present for the prosecution's case.

James Wilson, another gang member, cut a deal and testified for the prosecution's case against Hodges.[107] Wilson was in Placerville when the first robbery attempt was aborted. He opted out of going for the actual robbery. But his eyewitness testimony of the gang's activities and events leading up and following the Bullion Bend robbery added to the prosecution's case against Hodges.

Wilson testified[108] he . . . *was at Hodges House in May and June and part of the month of July.* He named many of the gang members he knew personally. He disclosed the secret password for entrance was "Jackson." Then he explained the intent of the group's activities and Hodges' involvement.

> *We had come to rob the stages: about the 20th of June we had a conversation in reference to this business. Hodges was present. We talked about coming up here and taking this money or this bullion. Cannot recollect the language used.*
>
> *Hodges said he thought it was right. Said I could do as I pleased about going. He would not advise me either to go or stay. This bullion was to be used for recruiting men to go to the South to keep the South fight the Federal Government to pay mens passage back.*
>
> *The parties I have named first met at Preston Hodges House. When I first got there Jim Grant and George Baker were there. Ingram came somewhere in the forepart of May. Hodges knew where we were going from the start. He said we were right, that they were robbing our people back at home and it was just and right that we should retaliate.*

Wilson continued his testimony with more details.

Hodges furnished provisions while we were in his neighborhood. Pool and others started from his house on this expedition in June. Ingram and Clendening asked Hodges if I was going. He said he thought not. Then they asked me, and I told them I was not going. John Clendening asked me. Hodges was there at the time.

After they got off on the second trip, I next saw them at Hodges. Clendening, Baker, Glasby and Bulwer came there. Hodges went to town and got some clothes for them — that is for Glasby and Bulwer. They came on Saturday. Bulwer and I went hunting that day and Glasby stayed at the place. On Saturday night I think it was I took them over on what is called the Arroyo Hondo. After that I took provisions to them at Hodges request before the expedition.

When the party started on the last expedition they were at Hodges house late in the evening. I was in bed . . . they were going to rob the Stages of Wells Fargo & Co — that was well understood. Hodges was present when they said that. They ate supper there.

When Hodges gave me the $10, he only lent it to me. Grant was to repay him out of the money Baker gave him for our expenses. These men did not pay for the provisions Hodges furnished. Hodges told me they were to pay him. They were to let him have money to pay for his trouble — to go down to Mazatlan to live — him and his family. Heard him and Grant talking about the horse he let Grant have after the party drove him off — about trading it away.

This company was first raised to back the South to oppose the Federal arms. The head men of the party said so — Baker and Ingram.

Wilson recounted, . . . *the last month I have been in prison in San Francisco, San Jose, Sacramento, and Placerville since last night. Sheriff Van Eaton brought me up last night. In prison at Sacramento four weeks, fifteen days at San Francisco and four or five days at San Jose.*

He added, *I left Hodges house before my arrest at his request and his wife. She was scared and thought I had better leave and I did so. I don't know whether they were scared on my account or afraid of being arrested themselves. Had no hostile or angry feelings against them for it. They did not talk unkindly at all. It was their privilege and right. I was not afraid to stay there but they wanted me to leave. I did not make any objection against going. My object in joining this expedition was to aid the South. Never told any man I intended to make my fortune out of it.*

Finally, on redirect, Wilson stated: *There had been a good deal of talk and hard feeling in the community against Hodges on account of his keeping these men at his place —and Mrs. Hodges was scared and thought I had better leave. Hodges thought I had better go down in the Valley and stop awhile.*

The prosecution also called Al Glasby to testify and provide details of Hodges' involvement in the planning and aftermath of the Bullion Bend robbery. When Glasby completed his testimony for the prosecution, his credibility was attacked by the defense counsel.

The attorney asked, *Are you still in custody?* Answer: *Yes, I am. Right here in the Placerville jail.* Glasby admitted he expected to be freed after the trial. Question: *So you've traded the truth for your freedom, isn't that right?* Objection sustained! Question: *Mr. Glasby, let's put it this way. You understand the charges against you will be dropped after this trial, and that's in consideration for your testimony here and at Mr. Poole's trial. That's correct, is it not?* Answer: *Yes, it is.*[109]

The prosecution called two more witnesses: Thomas Ogan and John M. Ogan. They were Hodges' Santa Clara County neighbors. They had seen the men in question near Hodges' ranch and added, *sometimes the men were armed.*[110]

After the prosecution's case rested, the defense called several witnesses to the stand. They were primarily Hodges' friends, neighbors, and old acquaintances. They included: William Easch, Art Hopper, William Overfeldt, George McCracken, Henry Phelps, Daniel McRae, David Lundy, Thomas Maxey, and Robert M. Phelps. Collectively, they testified about Hodges: . . . *his character as a peaceable, quiet, law abiding citizen was now and always had been above reproach.*[111] Thomas Bodley testified, *Hodges conduct during the six or seven years I have known him has been that of a peaceable law-abiding citizen.*[112]

PRESTON HODGES WAS LABELED AS A RIGHTEOUS UPSTANDING CITIZEN. BUT HE DID NOT TAKE THE WITNESS STAND.

After counsel's concluding remarks, Judge Brockway essentially gave the jury the same instructions as in Poole's trial. They were then excused to deliberate the case's merits.

Unlike Poole's jury, the deliberations must have been difficult. The jurors were out for a long time. The hours drug by. The courtroom clock seemed to stand still.

After twenty hours, one juror requested more information and direction from the judge. Fifteen minutes later, the jury returned and announced their verdict in court. Here's what the newspaper reported.

Hodges Found Guilty. – Placerville, Sept. 10 – 1:20 P.M. – *The jury in the case of Preston Hodges, after being out twenty hours, returned a verdict of guilty of murder in the second degree.*[113]

Both men, Thomas B. Poole and Preston Hodges had been tried and convicted. The judge called a recess to consider the two men's sentences.

The courtroom clock continued to tick away the hours.

9

TRIBULATIONS

That evening, the news was swift for Thomas Belle Poole.

> **Pool Sentenced to Be Hung.** – Placerville, Sept. 10, 6:30 P.M. – *Thos. B. Pool, the Confederate stage robber, was to-day sentenced by Judge Brockway to be hung on the twentieth-day of October. This being the last day of the term, Hodges will be sentenced this evening.*[114]

For an hour and a half, Preston Hodges sat in his jail cell. Tom Poole was already sentenced to hang. What might Preston have been thinking? How heavy were his legs as he climbed the stairs to enter the courtroom? As he was escorted to his chair, what did he anticipate would happen?

The newspaper reported extensively on the conclusion of his case. This account[115] contains many lurid details of this courtroom drama. They are extensive and important to digest completely.

> **Sentence of Hodges.** – Placerville, Sept. 12, 1864
> *Justice has been swift to overtake the expedition which left the quiet Valley of Santa Clara to inaugurate civil war, with all its horrors, within the borders of our peaceful State. There remains of the gang –who took their departure from the house of Hodges with his "God be with you" — only two that are at liberty.*
>
> *They are indicted and branded as murderers. Two met their deaths at the hands of the officers. One is now under sentence of death. Another is consigned to a felon's cell for twenty years, and the balance, principals and accessories, are now occupants of our county jail, and the delay of meting out justice to them will be brief. The way of the transgressor is hard, indeed.*
>
> *The jury, as I telegraphed the Alta, returned a verdict of "guilty of murder in the second degree" against Preston Hodges, who "aided and abetted" the fitting out of the expedition; and at the hour of eight P.M. the prisoner was brought up from his cell to receive his sentence from Judge Brockway.*

As Preston Hodges sat down, he faced the man in whose hands his fate rested. The presiding judge, Samuel W. Brockway, of the 11th District Court pronounced his sentence for Preston Hodges with dramatic flair worthy of a politician. In extraordinary detail, he tongue-lashed the convicted man.

> *Preston Hodges, you were indicted by a Grand Jury of the County of El Dorado for the crime of murder, committed by the killing of Joseph Staples. Upon that indictment you were arraigned in the Court and entered a plea of 'not guilty.'*

> *You have been tried by a jury of your own selection, and after a trial in which you were defended by most able and earnest counsel of your own choice, the jury have returned a verdict finding you guilty of murder in the second degree. Have you now any legal cause to show why the judgment of the law should not be pronounced against you?*
>
> *The crime for which you were indicted and of which you have been convicted, is one of the highest known to the law. Its magnitude, when taken in connection with the circumstances developed upon your trial, which tend irresistibly to show you guilty of a crime of a degree even higher than the one for which you were indicted, is certainly of a startling character.*
>
> *Upon all of the proof the jury found you guilty only of murder in the second degree; had their verdict been 'guilty of murder in the first degree,' the Court would have been quite satisfied with their finding. The evidence such as to justify a verdict of that character; the evidence seemed clearly under the law to establish your guilt of the great offence. Nor does your guilt stop even at the crime of murder; the evidence shows you to have been guilty of the highest crime known to our laws — treason to our common country.*

Judge Brockway clearly expressed his dissatisfaction with the second-degree murder conviction verdict. But then he moved into expanded territory with his remarks.

> *The evidence upon your trial shows you to have been acting in concert with other parties in proposing, raising, fitting out, arming and organizing expeditions to wage war against the lawful authorities and Government of the State of California and of the United States. That you gave to such expeditions your counsel and approval — yes, that you gave*

money and means to assist in their organization and equipment there is no doubt.

You told the parties actively engaged in carrying out the purposes of the organizations, that to rob for the purpose of raising means to equip and form them, and pay their expenses to joining those are now waging war against our General Government, was no crime — that it was right and just: you bid them 'God speed'; you aided them; you counseled them; you encouraged them, and when they started upon the felonious expedition which resulted in the death of Staples, you piloted them on their way.

They were to rob and plunder, and if an arrest was attempted to resist it to the death. You were to remain quietly at your home, and on their return share the booty with them. With the means acquired by robbery and murder you were to recruit more men and increase the ranks of the guerrillas; you were to wage war against the United States and incite insurrection and civil war in the State of California.

In carrying out the common purposes of your organization, those whom you had sent forth upon the expedition to rob, plunder and, if need be, murder, killed a quiet law-abiding citizen — an officer of the law — engaged in their pursuit and seeking their arrest. This was murder, and the hands that armed them and sent forth the band were stained with blood; would it not have fully justified a jury in finding you guilty of murder in the first degree? — of it there is scarcely room to doubt. It was a felonious expedition, and all engaged in it were alike guilty of murder, whether engaged at the scene of the crime or at their homes, enjoying the protection of the law they were violating.

Next, Judge Brockway discussed state and federal law.

The laws of this State provide that, 'If any person shall within the limits and jurisdiction of this State begin, or set on foot, or propose, or furnish the means for, or knowingly aid or abet, or be concerned in beginning, setting on foot, or providing, proposing, or furnishing the means for any military or hostile expedition to be carried on against the Government of the United States, or the loyal citizens thereof, or their property, every person so offending shall be deemed guilty of felony,' and may be punished by death, provided a jury by their verdict shall determine and direct.

This is a wise and salutary provision of the law, intended to protect the citizens and preserve the State from civil war and bloodshed. This law you violated in its every principle. Had your purposes been carried out, civil war and insurrection would have been inaugurated in California; predatory bands of guerrillas would have roamed over the country, sacking towns, burning houses, murdering our people and drenching the land with blood; civil authority would have been inadequate to the protection of the people; war would have existed here in all of it most horrid forms — partisan, vindictive and malignant.

It is startling to contemplate the result had your purposes succeeded; such conspiracies are subversive of all law and endanger alike the public and private safety. It is the duty of all law-abiding citizens to suppress them — to expose all parties engaged in them and to aid the public authorities in bringing the guilty parties to punishment. These obligations you disregarded and gave the influence of your character to the commission of crime.

Providential circumstances arrest you in your guilty career, before it had culminated in open insurrection. Had you succeeded, the murder for which you have been tried and convicted would have been but a small particle in the great stain of crime and suffering you would have brought upon the State.

Next, Judge Brockway explained Preston Hodges' fate. He seemed to relish the details of what was in store for Hodges.

The law sought you out, witnesses established your guilt, and you must now suffer its just penalty. Well may you be thankful that your life is spared; yet the penalty you must suffer is terrible in its consequences to you. You are severed from the world, from friends, from your family, and in the prime of life ignominiously consigned to a felon's cell. No more may you enjoy the sweets of home or freedom — guilt has blasted your hopes forever. The law metes out to you its just punishment; bow in submission to its stern decrees and strive by earnest efforts to atone by a life of penitence and reformation for the great crime of which you are guilty. Do not indulge in the delusive hope of escaping from your punishment but devote the remainder of your life to seeking a reconciliation with him who can in all your afflictions soothe and sustain you, and who, if you be truly penitent, can make you happy even within the walls of a prison.

It but remains now for me to pass upon you the judgment of the law, which is: That you, Preston Hodges, be taken to the State's Prison of the State of California and be there confined at hard labor for the term of twenty years, to date from this day.

Judge Brockway clearly expressed his sentiments of what he believed had occurred. He wanted a stronger punishment for Preston Hodges. In his opinion, twenty years at hard labor in state prison was too lenient. A newspaper reporter offered this observation.

During the whole time the Judge was administering the sentence there was not a change of countenance or the exhibition of the least feeling on the part of the prisoner. He listened with interest and that was all. The fact that he is emphatically a Southern John Brown, and today believes himself a martyr to the cause of the South. He is a religious enthusiast of the high-key order. His letters to his wife, written whilst in jail, urged her 'to keep up the family altar,' etc. during his absence. It is said that he once offered up a prayer in the presence of this gang of murderers for their success before they set out on the expedition.

Preston Hodges' second degree murder conviction was official. His fate was a sentence of twenty years imprisonment at hard labor. Where? In the notorious California State Prison at Point San Quentin.

While his ranch house in the quiet Santa Clara Valley was only fifty miles south, it is hard to imagine how he could possibly be farther removed from his wife, Frances, and his children whom he loved so much. He had been separated from them for weeks. This stalwart Christian family man was now a convicted felon.

Three days removed from Judge Brockway's sentence in the El Dorado County Courthouse, what were his thoughts? In KGC castle meetings, the most risk Preston anticipated was as a military camp prisoner-of-war. What was ahead was far different than his desire to move his family to Mazatlán, Mexico.

As Preston approached his new abode — San Quentin — the infamous state penitentiary appeared on the horizon. On a windblown point just north of San Francisco, this place must have seemed so far away to him. He was being transported into another world. One with a bleak future indeed.

Physically and emotionally, San Quentin could not be farther from his youth's bucolic home.[117] He grew up at the foot of North Carolina's Blue Ridge Mountains' eastern slope.

San Quentin State Prison[116]
Courtesy of the California History Room, California State Library, Sacramento

Hodges cabin built in 1805 in Surry County, North Carolina
Courtesy of Bill Cole collection

When he set out from his North Carolina boyhood home as a young married man, could he ever have imagined this scenario? Probably not. Was twenty years at hard labor in San Quentin State Prison to be the fate of Preston Hodges?

Incarceration

On September 13, 1864, Preston Hodges was delivered to San Quentin State Prison. A local newspaper announced his arrival.

Marin County Journal.

SAN RAFAEL, SEPT. 17, 1864.

CONVICTS.—On Wednesday last, the Sheriff of Mendocino county passed through this place, on his way to San Quentin, having in charge three "beauties" for the State Hotel. We failed to learn their names, or for what crime they were convicted. On the day previous, Preston Hodges, one of the Placerville murderers and stage robbers, arrived and was locked up. He was sentenced for murder in the second degree, to imprisonment for the term of twenty years.

Marin County Journal, Town and Country column [118]
Courtesy of California State Library, CDNC

In the state prison clerk's office, Preston Hodges' incarceration began. The record that started this quest was most likely filled out on his desk.

For Preston and all other convicts, prison life began at 6:30 a.m. with a "get up" bell. Prisoners dressed, then triced up their bunks by hoisting them up and securing them with a rope. Then they stood at the door with their night buckets. When prisoners obediently conformed to the rules, the guards slid back bolts that secured their cells.

Convicts performed hard labor tasks mostly at the brickyard. Millions of bricks were manufactured during this period. They were used in the San Francisco building boom fueled by the Nevada silver mines and hydraulic gold mining in the El Dorado, which peaked in the early 1860s and lasted into the 1880s.

San Quentin State Prison Clerk's Office[119]
Courtesy of the California History Room, California State Library, Sacramento

Some days, the brickyard was hot and sweaty work. Other days, it was freezing cold due to the cool San Francisco Bay breezes. Even Mark Twain was known for his comments on the area's weather. He reputedly said, "The coldest winter I ever spent was a summer in San Francisco." However, that quote created much scholarly controversy. It appears he never actually said it.[120] But most agree with the sentiment expressed!

By the way, Mark Twain got into the act about this story. He filed a report on August 3, 1864, for the *San Francisco Daily Morning Call*. The headline was "More Stage Robbers and Their Confederates Captured." He mentioned Hodges by name.

During this period, San Quentin State Prison clothed inmates in striped uniforms. Mainstream prisoners wore vertical stripes. Horizontal stripes were for lifers. If prisoners got in trouble or were transported, they wore leg irons.

Prisoners routinely lined up for dinner at six o'clock. At nine o'clock, the light-out bugle sounded, and the guards secured the prisoners' cells for the night. Day after day and night after night the routine was the same.

On special occasions, some approved visits were allowed. The excursion steamer *Clinton* dropped off curious citizens, dignitaries, and even friends and family if allowed. No visitor records are available until the 1880s.

Year-End Drama

To close out 1864's memorable and dramatic events requires updates on several fronts. First, the legal wrangling began. Immediately upon Poole's conviction and Hodges' incarceration, the defense attorneys got to work. In October 1864, they appealed the murder convictions of both Thomas B. Poole and Preston Hodges.

On November 25, the California Supreme Court agreed to hear the appeal of both cases: "The People vs. Poole" and "The People vs. Hodges." The cases were scheduled in the court's first term in January 1865.

In early December, the *Daily Alta California* reported this tidbit about Wells Fargo & Company's legal involvement. *We understand that that house, having expended some $5,000 in the case already, will not employ counsel at any of the future trials, either in the cases pending in the Supreme Court, if new trials be granted, or those which are yet to be tried by Judge McKune. It is held by Wells, Fargo & Co. that the State and El Dorado county together should bear the burden of the further prosecution of the case, as the offence committed is one against the community at large.*[121]

Second, a Wells Fargo & Company profit and loss statement for the Express Department[122] details costs related to the "Washoe Stage Robbery." For this same robbery, the moniker "Bullion Bend" emerged later as it blossomed into legendary status. The 1864 year-end financial report provides robbery expense details this author had not seen reported elsewhere.

From public newspaper reports, the company engaged three attorneys in the Placerville trials — J.C. Goods; N. Greene Curtis; and McShafter — all from San Francisco. Financial expenditures listed show J.C. Goods received $645.00 for his services. Another line item "Attorneys in cash Washoe" lists $1,175.00 paid. Those legal fees equal $1,820.00

Another bank received $534.85; a dry goods company received $700.00; and one company received $2,250.00 which appears to be a reimbursement for stolen gold coins.

Rewards for the killing or capture of three robbers in San Jose total $1,500.00 or $500.00 each. A $500.00 line-item appears to be another reward. And $1,790.75 is listed as "Rewards July."

"August expenses" are $702.50, and "Sheriff Expenses" are $263.08. These robbery line-item expenses total $12,726.46. However, an additional item is specified: "Silver Bar lost Washoe stage" with a value of $1,944.08.

In round numbers, Wells Fargo accounted for almost $15,000 in robbery-related expenses. Compared to a potential loss of stolen loot valued from $40-80,000, that appeared to be a good investment. But in early December, Wells Fargo & Co. figured their return on investment was not worth further expenses. Most reports indicate the stolen loot was entirely recovered. Of course, that did not squelch the rumors of buried treasure which persist into modern times.

Third was the political front. For the first time since 1812, a presidential campaign unfolded in wartime. For much of 1864, Lincoln himself believed he would not be re-elected. Republican dissidents, the "Radical Republicans," formed the Radical Democracy Party. They nominated Californian senator and 1856 Republican presidential candidate, John C. Frémont, as their presidential candidate. Frémont withdrew on September 22nd and endorsed Lincoln. The country was war-weary. But with the Confederate states ineligible, only twenty-five Union states voted.

On November 8, President Lincoln won re-election over Democratic candidate George B. McClellan. McClellan ran as the "peace candidate" who wanted to bring the American Civil War to a speedy end through a negotiated settlement.[123]

Even though the South's demise appeared inevitable to some, a fourth area — the war front — was most influential in shaping the attitudes of the times. Upon hearing the news of Lincoln's re-election, General William Tecumseh Sherman ordered 2,500 Army light wagons loaded with supplies. On November 15, his troops burned the industrial section of captured Atlanta. One witness reported, ". . . immense and raging fires lighting up whole heavens . . . huge waves of fire roll up into the sky; presently the skeleton of great warehouses stands out in relief against sheets of roaring, blazing, furious flames." Seventy-five years later, the famous Atlanta burning movie scene in *Gone with the Wind* etched these images into the public's collective consciousness. That day, Sherman's destruction of Georgia had begun. His troops moved out to begin the famous "March to the Sea" which wreaked havoc on the countryside. On December 21, they captured the port city of Savannah.[124] General Sherman sent a short telegram to Abraham Lincoln the following day. It said, *I beg to present you as a Christmas gift the city of Savannah with 150 heavy guns and plenty of ammunition and also about 25,000 bales of cotton.*[125]

A new year was just around the corner.

10
1865

The year began eventfully for two Bullion Bend convicted prisoners. In Placerville's jail, Tom Poole awaited news anxiously. In San Quentin, so did Preston Hodges.

On Tuesday, January 3, California Supreme Court's session started. *Motions and examinations for license to practice as attorney and counsellor*[126] were attended to during the court opening. On the next day, case number 495, The People vs. Thomas Pool, came up third on the docket. Case number 518, The People vs. Hodges, was seventh.

Tom Poole's appeal claimed he was denied a fair trial in Placerville and should be given a new one. The Attorney General of the State of California appeared on behalf of the People. Poole was represented by his attorney, James Johnson.[127]

Each objection filed by Poole's counsel was addressed by the court. A few key statements shed light on their ruling.[128]

First, after reviewing evidence of deputy Staples' killing, the court concluded:

> *The testimony, taken as true, established the fact that the defendant was a conspirator with others to commit the crime of robbery, and to resist apprehension therefore even to the taking of life, was concerned in the unlawful killing of the deceased, Joseph M. Staples, while in the discharge of his duty as a peace officer in the County of El Dorado, and that the circumstances of the homicide showed that the act was done with an abandoned and malignant heart.*

Second, the court addressed the district court judge's jury instructions. In defining first-degree murder, Judge Brockway substituted the word "or" in place of the word "and." The statue defines it as a "willful, deliberate and premeditated killing." The court addressed this as a "mild designation" and dismissed it.

Attorney Johnson's argument that the prosecution failed to prove Poole fired the fatal bullet was also not an issue. The court noted, . . . *being confederated together for the felonious purpose of robbery and resistance to the civil power of the State, the killing of the deceased, by whichever of them, was an act of each and all of the conspirators.*

When other arguments were also dismissed, the court affirmed the conviction of Thomas B. Poole. It ruled, *Upon the case presented, there cannot be a shadow of doubt that the prisoner was in fact guilty of murder in the first degree.*

For case 518, The People vs. Preston Hodges, the defendant's attorney, J.W. Williams, submitted several detailed legal points in his arguments. During the El Dorado County trial, eyewitnesses testified that Preston Hodges was not in the county when and where the crime was committed.

If the jury had convicted Hodges of first-degree murder, the aiding and abetting of the gang either before or after the crime could have been tied to that specific verdict. But Preston Hodges was convicted of a lesser charge. That fact gave the El Dorado County court no legal and jurisdictional right to try him. Hodges was not in the county to commit the crime for which he was accused. Therefore, the Supreme Court had no choice but to overturn the lower court's verdict. This basic rule of law was either overlooked or ignored.

In his appeal's conclusion, J.W. Williams eloquently and simply cut directly to the legal heart of the matter. *The consciences of the jurors could not be so far misguided, as to permit them to bring in a verdict of guilty in the first degree, although, if the theory of the prosecution (evidently adopted and enforced by the county) that the killing of Staples was murder in the first degree, be correct, Hodges is guilty, either, of that crime or of none.*[129]

The California Supreme Court judges agreed. They ruled, "As it is apparent on the face of the record that the whole of the proceedings was 'coram non judice,' the judgment cannot be permitted to stand, even though the motion in arrest was not, in terms, based upon that objection." In non-legal terms, the court confirmed that Preston Hodges was tried in the wrong jurisdictional county for his convicted crime.

The court ordered the "judgement reversed and cause remanded." This effected Preston Hodges' release from San Quentin. But his legal battle was far from over. On February 20, the Placerville court complied with the California Supreme Court ruling in The People vs. Preston Hodges. This is the El Dorado County court order:[130]

El Dorado County Court Record, Feb. 20, 1865
Bill Cole collection

Its transcription:

The People of the State of California
    against
Preston Hodges

On this the 20th day of February AD 1865. A Remittitur from the Supreme Court reversing the Decision and Judgment heretofore rendered in this cause — being on file — It is Ordered: That the Sheriff of the county of El Dorado remove said defendant Preston Hodges from the State Prison of this said State. And deliver him into the custody of the Sheriff of the county of Santa Clara Third Judicial District — and that said Defendant Preston Hodges be there held upon a charge of Murder until legally discharged — It appearing from the Evidence upon the trial of said Defendant in this court that he is guilty of the crime of murder as charged by the Indictment pending herein — the venue for the trial of which is in said county of Santa Clara

John C. Butler	Peff
vs	
C. J. Roussin	Deft

THE COURT ORDER MADE IT VERY CLEAR WHAT IT BELIEVED. PRESTON HODGES WAS GUILTY OF MURDER.

Within days, Preston Hodges' scenery changed. He was transported from the windblown state prison on a point in San Francisco Bay to the Santa Clara County Jail in downtown San Jose. A newspaper reported[131] on February 24, Preston Hodges was *today admitted to bail in the sum of $5,000, at San Jose, to appear next Wednesday for examination.* The courthouse stood at the southeast corner of Second and San Fernando Streets. The brick jail had been completed in 1855. It was considered remarkably secure for confining prisoners.[132]

Some other gang members joined him there. *In view of the Supreme Court ruling, the other defendants were also returned to San Jose, where their Copperhead companions posted $4,000 bail for each of them.*[133]

Preston's bail was twenty-five percent higher than his companions. The authorities obviously viewed him as the gang's de facto leader and assigned his bail more risk. While KGC's militia, political, and financial influence diminished as the war drug on, it's fair to assume the local area Copperheads' coffers were not empty.

On March 15, the *Marysville Daily Appeal* provided additional details regarding Santa Clara County's ongoing legal process.

The Placerville Stage Robbers. –

On the final examination of the Placerville prisoners, before Judge Thomas, says the San Jose Mercury, Preston Hodges was held as accessory to the murder of Sheriff Staples. He was admitted to bail in the sum of $15,000 to appear for trial at the District Court.

Robinson, Jarboe, and Grant were held for treason, under the statute of 1863. The first two were admitted to bail in the sum of $8,000 each.

The balance of the party, with the exceptions of Wilson and Glasby, who were detained as witnesses, were discharged, there being, really, no evidence against them, by which they could by any probability be convicted.[134]

Upon Glasby's release, the sheriff "encouraged" Alban Harvey Glasby to immediately leave California and never come back. As they say in the westerns, he was told to "get out of Dodge." But the newspaper also reported that the court *found trays and indictments against Jim Grant, Robinson (sic) and Wilson.* But it switched gears on one prisoner. *Grant was instead convicted of grand larceny and on April 3 entered San Quentin to serve a two-year sentence.* [135]

In the midst of this California legal wrangling, what else was going on? Let's consider the nation's larger scope of events.

On March 25, Lincoln expressed his sentiments about California to a friend. *I have long desired to see California; the production of her gold mines has been a marvel to me, and her stand for the Union, her generous offerings to the Sanitary Commission, and her loyal representatives have endeared your people to me; and nothing would give me more pleasure than a visit to the Pacific shore, and to say in person to your citizens, 'God bless you for your devotion to the Union,' but the unknown is before us. I may say, however, that I have it now in purpose when the railroad is finished, to visit your wonderful state.*[136]

Lincoln's remarks about California's "stand for the Union" seem ironic given the local Copperheads' fervor. But Lincoln's generous spirit was real. His desire to heal the nation's wounds was paramount. He believed with all his heart that unity in the United States of America was soon-to-be possible.

On March 27 just two days later, Lincoln met his two key generals, Grant and Sherman, at City Point, Virginia. They assured Lincoln the war's end was close and plotted the strategy for its swift end.

The agenda included the terms of surrender. President Lincoln wanted his generals to clearly understand what he wanted to happen. "He stressed that any surrender terms must preserve the Union war aims of emancipation and a pledge of equality for the freed slaves."[137]

But equally important was Lincoln's concern to reconcile the nation. When the moment of Lee's inevitable surrender came, Lincoln stressed to Grant there would be no more Northerners and Southerners. There were only to be Americans. Once again, Lincoln wanted the country to be the "United" States of America.

Within a week, the Union Army's forces closed in on the outmanned and outgunned Southern forces. On April 9, the Civil War effectively ground to a halt. Gen. Robert E. Lee's forces surrendered to Gen. Ulysses S. Grant, commander of the Union Army, at Appomattox Courthouse.

As instructed by Lincoln, Grant sincerely extended care to the vanquished Southern forces. The two opposing generals, Grant and Lee, worked together on the smallest details. An onsite printing press immediately generated vouchers for the Southern soldiers. They were to lay down their arms and go home by any available means of transportation. Mutual respect was extended to individual soldiers who had fought valiantly in this bitter war. Only days before, they were sworn enemies.

A domino effect cascaded from Lee's surrender. *It marked the disbandment of the Army of Northern Virginia with the parole of its nearly 28,000 remaining officers and men, free to return home without their major weapons but enabling men to take their horses and officers to retain their side arms/pistols, and effectively ending the war in Virginia. This event triggered a series of subsequent surrenders across the South.*[138]

Four days later, on April 11, Lincoln gave an impromptu speech from his White House balcony window to the crowd gathered outside. The president reiterated how he favored granting suffrage to former slaves. In the crowd, a KGC knight — actor John Wilkes Booth, listened attentively. Booth declared it would be the last speech that Lincoln would ever make. The course of history was about to change.

Three days later was Good Friday, April 14. President and Mrs. Lincoln attended an evening play at Ford's Theater. During the performance, the heavy weight and toll Lincoln carried began to lift with laughter. Suddenly, John Wilkes Booth emerged from the shadows and fired a shot into the back of Lincoln's head. Booth leapt onto the stage and shouted, *Sic Sempre Tyrannis*. Its translation from Latin is, *Thus always to tyrants*. Reputedly uttered by Brutus in 44 BC when he slayed Julius Caesar, it is also the state motto of Virginia, Wilkes' home state.

UPON HEARING OR READING THE NEWS OF
LINCOLN'S ASSASSINATION, MOST OF THE NATION WEPT.
BUT NOT ALL.

Some Southern loyalists cheered when they heard the news. As far away as Paris, celebrations were held. Reports that people jumped with glee and clicked their heels were widely circulated. These Copperheads did not follow Lincoln's spirit of reconciliation and grace he extended to the vanquished Southern troops at Appomattox and beyond. Sad but true.

It's hard to know the hearts and minds of people. How would any of us have reacted to this chain of events? In these tumultuous times, a person's upbringing and values formed what beliefs were held dear. What else did someone cling to? The whipsaw, whiplash, and compounding layers of each event — one upon the other. The emotional toll must have been nearly unbearable. From a Santa Clara County publication, we gain this local perspective.

> *When the news of the assassination of Abraham Lincoln reached San Jose, there was at first a stillness as if the population had been stricken with mental paralysis. Then excitement grew until it reached fever heat.*
>
> *The residents were composed of two elements, the northerners and the majority of the westerners who upheld the cause of the Union; and the southerners and southwesterners, who sympathized with the cause of the Confederacy.*
>
> *Good, honest men on each side, but divided in opinion by the effect of early environment. Among the Confederate sympathizers were many of San Jose's prominent men. In the country districts the same conditions prevailed. While the excitement over the death of Lincoln was at its height some of the southerners were so indiscreet as to publicly express their joy over the death of a man who had been pictured to them as a human gorilla and a negro lover.*
>
> *The Union men were in a majority and whenever an anti-Union sentiment found utterance the speaker was quietly placed under arrest. Several prominent citizens were conveyed to Alcatraz prison, San Francisco Bay, but their term of imprisonment was short, for after partisan bitterness had been partially allayed their release was ordered and they came back to their farms and business.*[139]

Understandably, it would be a long time before people would move past these deep wounds. Some argue the nation's wounds still haven't healed more than a century and a half later. Recent examples of Confederate flags and monuments being lightning rods for conflict indicate more healing is required.

But the California legal drama related to Bullion Bend and its aftermath was far from over.

Pleas to Pardon Tom Poole

As Tom Poole's execution date approached, many letters were received by Governor Frederick Low supporting a pardon or leniency for Tom Poole. Several surprising letters were written on his behalf. One was from George Ranney, the deputy sheriff wounded in the Somerset House gun battle with the robbers.

Another letter received was from Deputy Sheriff J.D. Van Eaton. Not only was he a member of the posse that chased the gang, but he extracted Poole's confession in jail. About Poole he wrote:

> *He gave me the names of his associates, told me that they came from Santa Clara County and that they would be apt to stop either there or at Kings River near Visalia, and gave me the names of parties near Visalia who could inform me where their camp might be found if they should happen to be there.... Without the information thus given it is not probable that we would ever have succeed in recovering the last three bars of bullion that were found ... through information given by him the organization was entirely broken up.*

Seven jurors who convicted him of murder wrote letters asking for clemency. Former Judge James Johnson wrote two long letters — a four-pager and an eight-pager. He conducted extensive interviews with Poole and others after his conviction.

A few comments from this former judge are worth review. He wrote, *There is nobody who denies that the trial in the District Court was a complete farce. That, such is the fact, is cordially acknowledged by the District Attorney.*[140]

Wow! The trial was "a complete farce." What an incredible statement from a former judge who served eleven years on the bench!

Before being led to the scaffold, Tom Poole was interviewed for the last time by Johnson. This transcription is from Judge Johnson's final letter. The document is in Governor Low's Request for Pardon file.[141] Judge Johnson wrote:

A few hours after the letter of your Excellency reached me, I had my last interview with Poole. In that interview he said among other things and with much emphasis 'I am no murderer. I feel as if now, for the first time, I was about to be tried before a court of Justice.'

That Poole committed a robbery I do not deny. I think that I shall always believe his dying statement that he was 'NO MURDERER' was correct and regret that a man innocent of murder should be publicly executed.

But your Excellency has concluded that a faithful execution of the laws forbade even the granting of a respite and however much I regret the decision I must acquiesce.

Respectfully your obt (sic - obedient) Servant (signed) James Johnson

In a descriptive *California Police Gazette* article, *Poole said he felt extremely grateful to Sheriff Rogers, deputies Hume and Van Eaton, and the jailer, Mr. De Goha, for kind treatment during his long imprisonment. He said he was ready to die and had hope of a better world; during a few years he had belonged to a church; and that was the best and most useful portion of his life: the coolness with which he looked on death was neither mere nerve nor bravado —it came from within, from a sense of Divine support.*[142]

As Thomas B. Poole walked out into the jail courtyard, he saw the custom-built scaffold ahead. Did his mind's eye harken back to 1858, when he constructed the gallows to hang Jose Anastasio in Monterey County? The *Sacramento Daily Union* filed this report on Tom Poole's execution:

At 12 o' clock precisely, he calmly ascended the scaffold, cordially shook each person by the hand, and fearlessly resigned his spirit to God. He smiled on all and seemed perfectly resigned. He died almost without a struggle and in a few seconds.[143]

As a footnote, Poole's son later claimed that his father's appeal for a pardon from Governor Low was refused not only because *times were too hot* during the Civil War. The other reason was because Tom Poole had executed Jose Anastasio in the face of the technical oversight of Governor Weller's reprieve.

In Wells Fargo Detective James Hume's biography, author Richard Dillon stated that Hume came to respect Poole after the trial. Upon Poole's execution by hanging, he wryly commented:[144]

"HUME FELT IN CIVIL WAR CALIFORNIA TWO WRONGS DID, APPARENTLY, MAKE A RIGHT."

11
PRESTON HODGES' SAGA CONCLUDES

As Tom Poole awaited execution, the legal system finally ground to a conclusion on the other cases. With the war over, many people were ready to put the past behind them — in terms of Civil War actions. Lincoln's spirit of reconciliation took hold in some places.

In Santa Clara County, all charges against Preston Hodges and his cohorts were dismissed. Newspapers still considered it relevant.[145]

In short order on September 13, the attorneys filed for *said defendants to be discharged from custody.* A demurrer[146] was filed on September 14. The district judge sustained the demurrer and set aside the indictment.

An order for the defendants' discharge was issued on September 18. A newspaper reported, *Washington Jordan, Wallace Clendenning, John Ingram and Cross, Gamble, and*

> THE PLACERVILLE STAGE ROBBERS.—The San
> Jose *Mercury* of September 12th has the following:
>
> The recent wholesale discharge, by our District Court, of the parties in this county indicted for the murder of Sheriff Staples, has elicited no little comment by the press throughout the State. Several journals have censured the San Jose papers for their reticence on the subject. We merely mentioned the circumstance of the discharge, at the time, without comment, inasmuch as the only case wherein the Court had discretion was that of Preston Hodges, and an appeal having been taken in his case to the Supreme Court, we preferred to remain silent, at least until the final decision should be rendered. There were two indictments against Preston Hodges, one for the murder of Sheriff Staples, another for treason. Upon the latter indictment counsel for the prisoner filed a demurrer, which was sustained by Judge McKee. The demurrer set forth that the District Court had no jurisdiction of the offense named, in that it appeared that the crime therein charged is an offense against the Government and laws of the United States, and only cognizable in the Federal Courts, and on the further ground that if any State Court had jurisdiction it was the County Court. The Court ordered the indictment to be set aside and the prisoner to be discharged. District Attorney Spencer filed a bill of exceptions to the rulings of the Court, and carried the case to the Supreme Court. For the crime of murder in this case, as well as in the cases of the others indicted for the same offense, the District Attorney was satisfied that he had no evidence to convict. As the prisoners were all within this county at the time the murder was committed in another part of the State, and as the evidence to prove them accessories before the fact was of a vague and untenable nature, he concluded to enter a nolle prosequi in their behalf rather than subject the county to the expense of a bootless trial. In this he doubtless acted advisedly.

Gately were all released when the district attorney decided he lacked sufficient evidence to convict them.[147]

On the 20th of September, Sheriff J.H. Adams signed a written confirmation that Undersheriff R.B. Hall had *personally served the written notice of appeal on Preston Hodges on the 23rd day of September by delivering to him a certified copy . . . and also to John A. Robinson (sic - Robertson) on the 20th day of September.*

Finally, the detailed appeal transcript filed on October 13, 1865. It closed the case for good.

With his conviction overturned, Preston Hodges was at last a free man. This photo is believed to be from the early to mid-1860s.[148] It fits the description of the newspaper reporter at his trial's beginning. It stated he was, *well-dressed, apparently well-to-do man, rather large sized, perhaps forty-five or fifty years old, with a florid face and very sandy beard and whiskers.* Since Preston was born in 1833, the reporter's only judgement error was to over-estimate Preston's age.

Preston Hodges c 1860s, *Courtesy of Sally Durst collection*

Another photo of Preston Hodges[149] is believed to be from the 1890s. What struck this author about his great-granduncle is that Preston is much thinner in the later photo. The physical differences certainly make sense. For five months, he served time at hard labor in San Quentin State Prison.

Within a year's time, he was in jail and transported as a prisoner three times. When bailed out of jail, it was only for a short time. After all, a reputed stagecoach robbery gang leader and convicted murderer would be closely monitored.

Preston Hodges c 1890s
Courtesy of Bill Cole collection

But relatively soon, some semblance of normal life began to return. His daughter, Amy, was born on August 25, 1866 — some eleven months after his Santa Clara County court case was dismissed and papers served.

In 1868, Preston applied for a land transaction based on the Homestead Act of 1862. All applicants swore an oath and pledged to support and defend the Constitution of the United States of America. This affidavit[150] bears his signature.

Preston would not have taken this pledge lightly. Guided by strong values and principles, this author and relative believes Preston sincerely pledged his loyalty. He would not lie. In fact, that may be the very reason why his defense attorneys did not put him on the witness stand. At age thirty-five, he was ready and anxious to put the trials of his past behind him. He prayed for a long life ahead to enjoy with his family.

PRESTON HODGES' SAGA CONCLUDES

AFFIDAVIT

To accompany Applications to purchase State Lands, as required by
Act of Legislature, passed April 27th, 1863.

I do solemnly Swear That I will support, protect, and defend the Constitution and Government of the United States against all enemies, whether domestic or foreign, that I will bear true faith, allegiance, and loyalty to the said Constitution and Government, any ordinance or law of any State, Convention, or Legislature, or any rule or obligation of any society, or association, or any decree or order from any source whatsoever, to the contrary notwithstanding, and that I will support the Constitution of the State of California; and further, that I do this with a full determination, pledge and purpose, without any mental reservation or evasion whatsoever, and that this oath is not taken for the purpose of acquiring title to, interest in, or possession of any land, in order that such title, interest, or possession, may be transferred to any person or persons to enable such person or persons to evade the provisions of any law of the State of California, or any regulation of the General Land Office at Washington.

Preston Hodges

Subscribed and sworn to before me, this *Twenty fifth* day of *April* 1868

Affidavit of Preston Hodges, Apr. 25, 1868
Courtesy, History San Jose

Another daughter, Lela Mae, was born on March 26, 1869. On June 29 just three months later, his wife, Frances, died of pneumonia. She was only thirty-two — within three weeks of her thirty-third birthday.

PRESTON'S LOSS OF HIS WIFE, FRANCES, WAS TRAGIC. IT CAME JUST FOUR AND A HALF YEARS AFTER HIS EXONERATION.

Frances' parents, Azariah and Elizabeth Lundy, with their five-year-old son in tow, arrived in San Jose in time for their daughter's funeral. They rode across country on the newly-completed transcontinental railroad. It was within two months of the golden spike ceremony.

Given the tragic circumstances, it's unlikely they enjoyed the amazing sights of buffalo herds, Native Americans, vast prairies, and majestic mountains right outside the train's windows. Their grief must have been intense. But they looked forward to joining their family. Most were already residing in California.

On January 1, 1871, Preston executed a land deed with his co-defendant, John A. Robertson, a successful merchant in San Jose. Robertson paid Hodges $500.00 in gold coins for this land.

In November of 1874, Preston Hodges became a founder of the Lompoc Colony in Santa Barbara County — located about two hundred miles south. One of forty investors, Preston moved there as the only one on-site. Except for one married daughter, his children moved with him. The family bonds were tight. Given the adversity faced in the previous decade, that's understandable.

This author believes other factors influenced Preston's move. The Bullion Bend robbery created much notoriety. For over a year, his name splashed across newspapers. Neighbors testified for the prosecution of his case. His Southern sympathies created tension in the community. He might have been ostracized. Perhaps his children were taunted by others. Starting over in a new location gave him a fresh start on life. A clean break with his past offered forward-looking possibilities.

Even though the Lompoc Colony's initial concept failed in just four years, Preston Hodges moved on effectively with his life and the lives of his family. He acquired 160 acres, farmed successfully, and operated the area's important steam threshing machine.

Preston never remarried. That's quite remarkable for a man in his thirties who lost his wife with eight children to raise. But he enjoyed his children and many grandchildren. Many of his descendants were born in Lompoc.

In 1905, Preston moved to Long Beach to live with his oldest daughter, Sarah, and her family. Recently, a newspaper advertisement surfaced.[151] It featured Preston's picture above this headline:

Catarrhal Throat Trouble Promptly Relieved

Mr. Preston Hodges, a retired farmer, now living at No. 2603½ San Pedro St., says: 'At the time I commenced treating at the Los Angeles Medical Institute I was bothered with a bad case of catarrh of the throat. I had all the bad symptoms: the tickling and constant desire to cough and clear my throat, the profuse expectoration, loss of appetite, in short, the usual symptoms of catarrh of the throat. I was attracted by the advertisements of the Los Angeles Institute, and determined to consult with these specialists, and now I am glad I did so, for my improvement began from the very first treatment, and I am more than please with what they have done for me and can safely recommend these physicians to any one in need of their services. I live at No. 2603½ San Pedro St. and will verify this statement to anyone interested. (Signed) Preston Hodges.'

He sounds like a satisfied customer. Or maybe it's just great marketing copy for the era.

On November 25, 1911, an unusual snippet was published in the *Los Angeles Daily Times*. On the same day this incident occurred, Hodges' grand-niece was born a few miles away in Downey. She happened to be this author's mother.

The newspaper reported, *Preston Hodges disappeared yesterday from the home of his sister on Rose avenue and was found this morning wandering on the beach in the vicinity of the inner harbor. He spent the night on the sand, sleeping in the open air.* From this, we can discern he might have experienced the onset of what would be labeled as dementia. In today's medical terminology, it could be Alzheimer's disease.

Preston Hodges died in 1913. One detail in his obituary[152] stood out: *during his last illness he loved to have his family pray with him and read to him from the Word of God.*

While what is written in his obituary is true, much is missing. There is no mention of Preston Hodges' entanglement with the Knights of the Golden Circle. Nor his involvement in Bullion Bend. Nor his El Dorado County murder conviction. Nor his San Quentin State Prison incarceration. Nor his case's overturned conviction ruling by the California Supreme Court. Nor his Santa Clara County charges of murder and treason. Nor his release and all charges dismissed.

FOR ALL FAMILY MEMBERS, HISTORIANS, AND GENEALOGISTS, LET THESE FACTS INSTRUCT US. THERE'S OFTEN MUCH MORE TO THE STORY THAN IS EASILY DISCOVERED.

> Preston Hodges died at the home of his daughter, Mrs. Sarah Parrent in Long Beach, February 18, 1913. He was born in Rockford, North Carolina, August 11, 1832, being 80 years, 4 months, and 7 days old. Before gaining his majority he was married to Miss Fanny Lundy, and with his young wife started west, arriving in San Jose, Santa Clara county, California in 1852. To this union were born seven girls and one boy, all of whom lived to adult age. In 1869 he lost his wife and from that time took upon himself the duties of both father and mother refusing to bring a step mother into his home. Two of his daughters preceeded him to the better land. The children living are, Mrs. Bell Ollinger, of San Francisco; Mrs. Lula Walker, of San Luis Obispo; Mrs. Lila Keesling, of San Jose; Mrs. Lizzie Lewis, of Los Angeles; and Mrs. Sarah Parrent, of Long Beach. W. A Hodges, his only son, lives at Lompoc. Preston Hodges was one of the early settlers in Lompoc, coming here in 1874. He bought the farm on which his son now lives and until about ten years ago was identified with every movement for the good of the community from its earliest settlement until he went to Los Angeles to live. During his last illness he loved to have his family pray with him and read to him from the Word of God, and expressed a willingness to go when the summons should come. His body was laid to rest in Signal Hill cemetery, Long Beach, there to await the resurrection of the just. Mr. Hodges was known and highly respected by all the old residents of Lompoc Valley and there are many here who sincerely mourn his death.

Obituary of Preston Hodges
Courtesy of Sally Durst collection

For the best of intentions, the real story might have been hidden from family members and friends. For good or bad, for better or worse, these facts were particularly important events in the life of Preston Hodges and his family.

As this author uncovered more and more of the story, he tracked down several descendants. Initially, none knew much — if anything — about these episodes in Preston's life. After a phone conversation asking about knowledge of Preston's San Quentin record, one descendant discovered a notebook filled with Richard Hughey's *Mountain Democrat* columns on the Bullion Bend robbery written in late 1999 to early 2000. The notebook, tucked away in a closet for years, was forgotten. But if any family members had direct knowledge of these events, the current generation knew nothing about this amazing and riveting true story.

Most certainly, the events chronicled in *Bullion Bend: Confederate Stagecoach Robbers, Murder Trials, and the California Supreme Court — Oh My!* . . . were not mentioned in Preston Hodges' obituary. But wouldn't it have been a shame to lose this treasure trove of historical and genealogical information?

Think of the storytelling possibilities at family meals and reunions from now on! Let's close with a question:

DO YOU REALLY KNOW THE FULL STORY OF YOUR RELATIVES?

BIBLIOGRAPHY

Primary Sources

Archives and Libraries

Amador County Archives, Sutter Creek
  Historical Files by individual
  Historical Photo collection

California State Archives, Secretary of State, Sacramento, California
  Governor's Offer of Reward, Aug. 4, 1864 (F3671:1:122)
  Governor's Prison Papers, Extreme Penalty Case File, Thomas Poole, 1865 (WPA1622)
  Lake Tahoe Wagon Road Map, 1895 (ID 58)
  San Quentin Prison Register, 1851-1867, Inmate No. 2820, Preston Hodges (microfilm, MF1:10(9))
  Secretary of State, Fee Book and Executive Record, 1858-1859 (F3639:4)
  Supreme Court Crim495, Peo. vs. Pool, 1865 (WPA569)
  Supreme Court Crim518, Peo. vs. Hodges, 1864 (WPA7000)
  Supreme Court Crim801, Transcript on Appeal, Peo. vs. Hodges, 1865 (WPA3019)

California State Library, Sacramento
  California History Room, San Quentin Photo Collection

California Police Gazette, Apr. 10, 1859

California Digital Newspaper Collection – accessed at the California State Library, Sacramento
   Daily Alta California, San Francisco, CA
   1864 - Jul. 2, 3, 17, 27; Aug. 27; Sep. 10, 11, 14; Dec. 4
   Daily Morning Call, San Francisco, California
   1864 - Aug. 3
   Marysville Daily Appeal, Marysville, California
   1864 – Aug. 24
   1865 – Feb. 25; Mar. 15
   Marin Journal, San Rafael, California
   1864 – Sep. 17
   Mountain Democrat, Placerville, California
   1864 - Jul. 2, 9, 23; Aug. 6, 20
   1865 - Sep. 30
   Pacific Sentinel, Santa Cruz, California
   1865 - Oct. 7
   Redwood City Gazette, Redwood City, California
   1864 – Jul. 29
   Sacramento Daily Union, Sacramento, California
   1864 – Jul. 2, 6, 7, 17; Aug. 5, 26, 27, 29; Sep. 8, 9, 10,
      12; Nov. 28; Dec. 29
   1865 – Feb. 7; Oct. 2, 16
   San Jose Mercury, San Jose, California
   1864 – Jul. 21; Aug. 4; Sep. 1

El Dorado County Historical Museum Archives, Placerville
   County District Court Minutes and Records, Feb. 20, 1864
   Historical Files by individual
   Historical Photo collection

History San Jose, San Jose
   Historical Files by individual
   Historical Photo collection

BIBLIOGRAPHY

Selected Secondary Sources
Books

Boessenecker, John. *Badge and Buckshot: Lawlessness in Old California* (Norman: University of Oklahoma Press, 1988)

Dillon, Richard. *Wells Fargo Detective*: *A Biography of James B. Hume* (New York: Coward-McCann, 1969)

Jerrett, Herman Daniel. *California's El Dorado Yesterday and Today* (Sacramento: Press of Jo Anderson, 1915)

Kearney, J.G. *Not of the Ruling Power: California's Fight in the Civil War* (Placerville: J.G. Kearney publisher, 2014)

Keehn, David C. *Knights of the Golden Circle: Secret Empire, Southern Secession, Civil War* (Baton Rouge: Louisiana State University Press, 2013)

Sawyer, Eugene T. *History of Santa Clara County, California* (Los Angeles: Historic Record Company, 1922)

Sioli, Paolo. *History of El Dorado County, California* (Oakland: Paolo Sioli publisher, 1883)

Trobits, Monika. *Antebellum and Civil War San Francisco: A Western Theater for Northern & Southern Politics* (Charleston: History Press, 2014)

Turner Publishing. *San Quentin Prison – 150th Anniversary.* (Turner Publishing, 2002)

Tuttle, Charles A., Reporter. *Pacific States Reports of Cases of California: The Supreme Court, Vol. 26.* (San Francisco: Bancroft-Whitney Company, 1906) p. 1055-7

Upton, Charles Elmer. *Pioneers of El Dorado* (Placerville: Charles Elmer Upton publisher, 1906)

Wilson, R. Michael. *Stagecoach Robberies in California: A Complete Record, 1856-1913* (Jefferson, North Carolina: McFarland & Company, 2014)

Woodward, Art. *The Westerners Brand Book* (Los Angeles: Los Angeles Corral, 1949)

Newspapers

Mountain Democrat, Series by Richard Hughey, columnist
    Bullion Bend Robbery: the true story. Nov 12, 1999
    Bullion Bend Robbery: part 3: Rufus Henry Ingram, the Red Fox. Nov. 22, 1999
    Bullion Bend Robbery: Preston Hodges and James Grant. Nov. 26, 1999
    Bullion Bend Robbery: Thomas B. Pool. Dec. 3, 1999
    Robbery at Bullion Bend: Gang plans its moves. Dec. 10, 1999
    The holdup at Bullion Bend occurs. Dec. 17, 1999
    The robbery at Bullion Bend: A Posse is formed at Placerville. Dec. 24, 1999
    Bullion Bend robbery: The bandits plan to rob the New Almaden stage. Jan. 7, 2000
    Bullion Bend robbery: The shootout at the Hill Ranch. Jan. 14, 2000
    The Trial of Thomas Bell Pool. Jan. 21, 2000
    Bullion Bend robbery: Charlie Watson testifies at Pool's trial. Jan. 28, 2000
    Bullion Bend robbery: Testimony of George Ranney at Pool's trial, part 1. Feb. 4, 2000
    Bullion Bend robbery: Testimony of George Ranney at Pool's trial, part 2. Feb. 11, 2000
    Bullion Bend robbery: Maria Reynolds testifies. Feb. 18, 2000
    Bullion Bend robbery: Alban Glasby testifies. Feb. 25, 2000
    Bullion Bend robbery: Preston Hodges' trial for murder. Mar. 3, 2000

Bullion Bend robbery: Glasby testifies against Preston Hodges, part 1. Mar. 10, 2000

Bullion Bend robbery: Glasby testifies against Preston Hodges, part 2. Mar. 17, 2000

Bullion Bend robbery: Pool and Hodges appeal to the Supreme Court. Mar. 31, 2000

Bullion Bend robbery: Placerville races to save Tom Pool. Apr. 7, 2000

Bullion Bend robbery: What have we learned? Apr. 14, 2000

San Francisco Post, May 7, 1887

Newspapers.com – accessed by Bill Cole, personal subscription
Los Angeles Daily Times, Mon. Dec 4, 1905
Los Angeles Daily Times, Sat. Nov. 25, 1911

Magazines

California Territorial Quarterly. No 51, Fighting Words. Chandler, Robert J. (Paradise: Bill & Penny Anderson. Fall 2002) p. 4-18

California Territorial Quarterly. No 88, The Mythical Johnston Conspiracy Revisited. Chandler, Robert J. (Paradise: Bill & Penny Anderson. Winter 2011) p. 18-36

Dogtown Territorial Quarterly. No 31, Democratic Turmoil. Chandler, Robert J. (Paradise: Bill & Penny Anderson. Fall 1997) p. 32-53

Private Collections

Bossenecker, John

Cole, Bill

Durst, Sally

Yamamoto, George

NOTES

Introduction
1. Matthews, Joe, Zocolo Public Square, Sacramento Bee, Viewpoints column, 7 January, 2016.
2. Ancestry.com, online accessed by Bill Cole, Sep. 9, 2015.
3. *An Act Concerning the Public archives*, Statutes of 1850, Chapter 1.
4. San Quentin Prison Register, 1851-1867, Inmate No. 2820, Preston Hodges (microfilm, MF1:10(9))
5. Bill Cole collection, Sep. 29, 2015.

Chapter 1
6. Photo 05658, El Dorado County Historical Museum.
7. http://www.malakoff.com/marshall.htm - James W. Marshall's account of the first discovery of the gold
8. https://www.loc.gov/rr/program/bib/ourdocs/Compromise 1850.html - accessed December 4, 2017
9. Azariah Lundy's diary transcribed, Bill Cole collection

Chapter 2
10. Keehn, David C. *Knights of the Golden Circle: Secret Empire, Southern Secession, Civil War*, p. 2
11. Myers, Jack. *Knight's Gold*. Jack O' Lantern Press, 2016
12. Woodward, Art. *Western Brand*. p. 74

13. http://knights-of-the-golden-circle.blogspot.com/ - accessed December 9, 2017
14. http://civilwar150th.blogspot.com/2011/04/lincoln-offers-lee-command.html, accessed Nov 12, 2017
15. citation
16. http://civilwar150th.blogspot.com/2011/04/lincoln-offers-lee-command.html - accessed Nov 12, 2017
17. https://www.raabcollection.com/abraham-lincoln-autograph/north-and-south-declarations-war - accessed Nov 16, 2017
18. *Dogtown Territorial Quarterly*, Number 31. Fall 1997, p 37
19. Library of Congress, Illus. in *Harper's weekly*, v. 7, no. 322 (1863 February 28) p. 144 (b&w film copy neg.)

Chapter 3

20. *San Francisco Post*, May 7, 1887 quoted Santa Clara County Under-sheriff, R.H. Hall
21. Diary of Azariah Lundy transcription, Bill Cole collection
22. Kearney, J.G. *Not of the Ruling Power*, p 68
23. No eyewitness recalled seeing Captain R.H. Ingram's Commission. Several testified they heard he presented it at a KGC meeting.
24. John Boessenecker collection
25. Gov. Weller's Executive Order, California State Archives
26. Governor's Reprieve entry for Jose Anastasio, Fee Book and Executive Record, Secretary of State (F3639:4, p. 48)
27. Ibid F3639.4
28. Ibid
29. Ibid
30. *Sacramento Daily Union*, Vol. 14, Mar. 6, 1858
31. Ibid
32. Woodward, Art. *The Westerners Brand* p. 73
33. *Mountain Democrat*. Richard Hughey column (RH) Nov. 26, 1999

34. *Mountain Democrat*. RH Nov. 26, 1999
35. Rambler, *San Francisco Post*, May 7, 1887 - also in Boessenecker p 138-9
36. Boessenecker p 137
37. Boessenecker p 137
38. *Mountain Democrat*. RH column, Nov 22 1999

Chapter 4
39. Chandler, Robert J., Wells Fargo Bank Historian retired, Bill Cole phone conversation Jan 2018
40. Tips for Stagecoach Travelers photocopied excerpts, Omaha Herald, 1877 – Historical Museum, Placerville, June 1988
41. LH0709, Autobiography and Reminiscence of James Mason Hutchings, San Francisco, 1901. The Society of California Pioneers.
42. Ned Blair photo courtesy of George Yamamoto collection. Author John Boessenecker believes this picture is not Ned Blair. Additional research is required.
43. Charley Watson photo courtesy of El Dorado County Historical Museum
44. James Grant photo courtesy of John Boessenecker collection

Chapter 5
45. Lake Tahoe Wagon Map segment, 1895, Courtesy of California State Archives
46. *Mountain Democrat*. RH Dec. 17, 1999
47. Ibid
48. Dillon. *Biography of James Hume.* p 90-92
49. Supreme Court (WPA569) People vs Tom Pool, Charley Watson testimony
50. Ibid
51. Ibid

52. Ibid
53. Ibid also Kearney. *Not of the Ruling Party*. p 49
54. Supreme Court (WPA569) People vs Tom Pool, Charley Watson testimony
55. Ibid
56. Ibid
57. Ibid
58. Ibid
59. Ibid, image from Bill Cole collection used with permission of CSA
60. Ibid
61. Supreme Court (WPA569) People vs Tom Pool, George Ranney testimony

Chapter 6
62. Supreme Court (WPA569) People vs Tom Pool, Alban Glasby testimony
63. Supreme Court (WPA569), People vs Tom Pool, George Ranney testimony
64. Ibid – also Maria Reynolds testimony
65. Charles Elmer Upton, *Pioneers of El Dorado*. Placerville: Charles Elmer Upton, Publisher, 1906. p. 138
66. Supreme Court (WP569) People vs Tom Pool, George Ranney testimony
67. Ibid
68. Upton, Charles Elmer. *Pioneers of El Dorado*, p. 134
69. *Mountain Democrat*. RH Feb. 11, 2000
70. Supreme Court (WPA569) People vs Tom Pool, George Ranney testimony
71. Supreme Court (WPA569) People vs Tom Pool, Glasby testimony
72. Supreme Court (WPA569) People vs Tom Pool, Maria Reynolds testimony
73. Ibid

74. Ibid
75. Ibid
76. Upton, Ibid 135
77. Upton, Ibid 134-5
78. *Mountain Democrat* photocopied article from Bob Jensen collection, El Dorado County Historical Museum
79. http://www.sacbee.com/news/local/crime/article 65499287.html
80. Find a Grave.com – accessed Oct. 29, 2015

Chapter 7

81. Boessenecker Ibid 149
82. Dillon, Richard. *Wells Fargo Detective: The Biography of James B. Hume*. 97
83. *California Police Gazette*, Oct. 7, 1865 also quoted in Dillon Ibid 97-8
84. Referenced by author J.G. Kearney p 64. Recollections of Van Eaton's grandson, Henry Bailey, and the stories his father told him
85. Dillon Ibid 98
86. Supreme Court (WPA569) People vs Tom Pool, Al Glasby testimony
87. Ibid
88. Ibid
89. Ibid
90. *Sacramento Daily Union*, Volume 27, 5 August 1864, City Intelligence article
91. *Mountain Democrat*. RH Jan 14, 2000
92. *Sacramento Daily Union*, Volume 27, 5 August 1864, City Intelligence article
93. Image Courtesy of El Dorado County Historical Museum - Courthouse on Main Street on right in front of Union St building 25
94. *Marysville Daily Appeal*. 24 August 1864

Chapter 8

95. *Mountain Democrat*. RH Jan 21, 2000
96. Ibid
97. Ibid Jan 21, 2000
98. Supreme Court (WPA569) People vs. Pool, Alban Glasby testimony
99. *Mountain Democrat*. RH Jan 21, 2000
100. Ibid
101. *Sacramento Daily Union*, Sep. 9, 1864
102. *Mountain Democrat*. RH Mar. 3, 2000 Preston Hodges' Trial for Murder
103. Supreme Court (WPA 7000) People vs Hodges, Al Glasby testimony
104. Supreme Court (WPA 7000) People vs Hodges, Thomas Pool testimony
105. Ibid
106. Ibid
107. Supreme Court (WPA 7000 People vs Hodges, Wilson, James testimony
108. Ibid
109. Supreme Court(WPA 7000) People vs Hodges, Alban Glasby testimony
110. *Sacramento Daily Union*, Sep. 10 1864 - The Placerville Highwaymen
111. Ibid
112. Supreme Court (WPA 7000) People vs Hodges, Thomas Bodley testimony p 42
113. *Daily Alta California*, Volume 16, Number 5305, Sep. 11 1864 by State Telegraph

Chapter 9

114. Ibid
115. *Daily Alta California*, Volume 16, Number 5308, Sep. 14, 1864

NOTES

116. San Quentin prison photographs album (HV9475.C3 S732 1907)
117. Built in 1805, the Bartholemew Hodges cabin is the ancestral home of the area's Hodges' clan. It is still in the family today. Preston's father, William H. "Buck" Hodges, is believed to have been born near this house, but it is not yet proven. Preston's father's farmland is only nine miles away. PC Hodges stated that his father never ranged outside of a nine-mile radius from where he was born. Photo Bill Cole collection
118. *Marin County Journal*, Town and Country Column, San Rafael Sep. 17, 1864
119. San Quentin prison photographs album (HV9475.C3 S732 1907)
120. https://www.anchorbrewing.com/blog/the-coldest-winter-i-ever-spent-was-a-summer-in-san-francisco-say-what-says-who/
121. *Daily Alta California*, Vol 16, No 5388, Dec. 4, 1864.
122. John Boessenecker collection
123. https://en.wikipedia.org/wiki/United_States_presidential_election,_1864
124. http://www.history.com/this-day-in-history/the-march-to-the-sea-begins
125. http://www.slate.com/blogs/the_vault/2012/12/20/william_tecumseh_sherman_s_gift_for_abraham_lincoln_1864_telegram_presenting.html - accessed Feb. 11, 2018

Chapter 10

126. *Sacramento Daily Union*, Vol 28, No 4297, Dec. 29, 1864 Supreme Court Calendar
127. *Mountain Democrat*. RH Mar. 31, 2000
128. Supreme Court (WPA569) People vs Tom Pool
129. Bill Cole's transcription of original document on file, California State Archives

130. Bill Cole collection photo, El Dorado Museum Archives, Old Court Minutes
131. *Marysville Daily Appeal,* No 46, Feb.25, 1865
132. Sawyer, Eugene T. *History of Santa Clara County California.* 1922. p 103-4
133. *Mountain Democrat.* RH Nov. 12, 1999
134. *Marysville Daily Appeal.* Mar. 15, 1865
135. Boessenecker, John. *Badge and Buckshot: Lawlessness in Old California,* University of Oklahoma Press, 1988. p 156
136. *CALIFORNIA IN TIME: The Fight Over Slavery through the Civil War.* Lincoln's remarks to Charles Maltby, Superintendent of Indian Affairs for California
137. http://www.history.com/this-day-in-history/lincoln-sherman-and-grant-meet
138. https://en.wikipedia.org/wiki/Battle_of_Appomattox_Court_House
139. Sawyer, Eugene T. *History of Santa Clara County California,* 1922. p 134
140. James Johnson letter, Gov. Low appeal for pardon of Tom Poole appeal California State Archives, Secretary of State, Sacramento, p. 7
141. Ibid, p. 8
142. *California Police Gazette,* photocopied article, John Boessenecker collection.
143. *Sacramento Daily Union.* Oct. 2, 1865
144. *Wells Fargo Detective,* p. 104

Chapter 11

145. *Sacramento Daily Union,* Volume 30 No 4545 The Placerville State Robbers 16 Oct 1865
146. Demurrer is a legal term valid in California law for an objection that an opponent's point is irrelevant or invalid, while granting the factual basis of the point.

NOTES

147. *Sacramento Daily Union*, Volume 30 No 4545 The Placerville State Robbers 16 Oct 1865
148. Photo, Courtesy of Sally Durst collection
149. Photo, Courtesy of Bill Cole collection
150. Affidavit, Courtesy of History of San Jose
151. *Los Angeles Daily Times*, Mon. Dec 4, 1905
152. Obituary of Preston Hodges, Courtesy of Sally Durst collection

INDEX

A

Adams, John Hicks (Sheriff), 73f, 124
    Hill Ranch posse, 73–75
Anastasio, Jose, 36, 122
Anderson, Robert (Major), 25

B

Baker, George H., 32, 75, 91
Band of 30, 24–25
Bickley, George W. L., Dr., 19
Biography of James B. Hume (Dillon), 71
Blair, Ned, 49f
    Bullion Bend stagecoach driver, 48–60, 52
    Somerset House, 64
Bodley, Thomas, 94
Boessenecker, John (author), 73
Booth, John Wilkes, 24, 118
Bouldware, John Creal, 39, 76, 87
Brady, Matthew, 29
Brockway, Samuel W. (El Dorado County Judge)
    arrests, 75
    change of venue, 82
    sentencing, 97–100, 102–103, 112
    trial, 87–88, 94
Bullion Bend robbery, 53–54, 54f
    Appeals, California Supreme Court, 111–121
    arraignments, 80–81
    arrests, 43, 64, 66, 75, 75t, 78
    Captain Ingram's Partisan Rangers, 53–60
    El Dorado County Court, trials, 82–103
    Governor Low, Bullion Bend robber rewards, 77, 77f
    Grand Jury warrants, 75–76
    Hodges ranch hideout, 72–73
    robbers pursuit of, 58–77
    Santa Clara County, trials, 114–116, 123–124
    Sheriff Adam's posse, 73–75
    Sheriff Roger's posse, 58–71
    Sheriff Van Eaton jail posing, 71–72
    Somerset House shootout, 61–66, 67f, 68f

stage coach robbery, 53–60
Staples funeral, 67, 67f
Bulware (see Bouldware)
Burke, Martin T. (San Francisco Police Chief), 59

C
California early history, 13–18
   1860 census, 21, 21t
   Gold discovery, 13–15
   population, 16, 16t
   Statehood, 15–16
California Police Gazette, 121
California State Archives, 7
California Supreme Court, trials
   attorneys, 112-113
   Hodges venue change, 113–115
   Poole appeal denied, 111–112
   Poole execution, 122
   Poole pardon pleas, 120–121
Captain Ingram's Partisan Rangers
   Bullion Bend stage coach robbery, 53–60
   Placerville stagecoach robbers, 43, 45
   planning additional robberies, 73
Cary House, Placerville, 79–80, 79f
Chandler, Robert J., Dr. (historian), 24, 29, 47
Civil War, 25–30
   additional states seceding, 28
   blockade, proclamation of war, 28
   California statement, 1865, 116
   casualties, 28, 29t, 30
   Fort Sumter, 25
   General Lee surrenders, 117
   Georgia attack by Sherman, 109
   Gettysburg, turning point, 30
   Lincoln, Generals 1865 meeting, 117
   Lincoln's post-war slavery speech, 118
   lingering national wounds, 119–120
   Militia Act, Lincoln call, 26
Clay, Henry (Senator), 16
Clemens, Samuel. *See* Mark Twain
Clennending, John, 39, 76
Clennending, Wallace, 39, 75, 78, 123
Cole, William E., vii
Compromise of 1850, 19
Comstock Lode, 20–21
Confederate Partisan Rangers. *See* Quantrill's Rangers
Copperheads, Confederate supporters, 1, 30f, 117–118
   bail posting, 115
   coffers, 115
   Hodges ranch, 88
   Knights of the Golden Circle (KGC), 38
   members, 29, 38
   Santa Clara County, 76
   Sheriff interruptions, 78
Cross, George, 38, 39, 75, 78
Curious teenager story, 57
Curtis, N. Greene (attorney), 108

D
Daily Alta California, 107
De Goha, Mr. (jailer), 121
Dillon, Richard
   Biography of James B. Hume, 71
   Poole execution critique, 122
Disunity over slavery, 19–30
   state secessions, 23, 23t

INDEX

E
Easch, William, 94
Edgerton, Carl (attorney), 80, 85
El Dorado County Court, 82, 83f
El Dorado County Court, trials, 82–103
   Hodges verdict, 94
   Hodges witnesses, 88–94
   Hodges sentencing, 98–103
   Hodges trial, 88–94
   Judge Brockway, 82
   jury selection, 86
   Poole sentencing, 97
   Poole trial, 85–88
   Poole verdict, 88
   Poole witnesses, 86–87
   venue change, 82
Emigrant Trail, Strawberry Valley, 46, 49
   Emigrant Train, 54f

F
Frear, James, 39, 75, 78, 82
Frear, Thomas, 39, 75, 78, 82
Fremont, John C. (Senator), 25, 108

G
Gamble, Joseph W., 39, 75-76, 78, 123
Gatley, John, 39, 75-76, 78, 124
Gelwicks, D. W. (publisher, Copperhead), 29
Genealogy chart (Hodges), 5f
Glasby, Alban Harvey, 42f
   Bullion Bend robbery, 55–60
   Capt. Ingram's Partisan Rangers, 41, 46
   capture, 74
   Grand Jury testimony, 75–76, 87–89
   imprisonment, 78–82
   Knights of the Golden Circle (KGC) recruitment, 41
   released from custody, 116
   report to Hodges, 72
   Somerset House, 61–64
   State's evidence, 87–93
   witnesses, 86, 86t, 89, 93
Gold discovery, 13–15
Goods, J. C. (attorney), 108
Grand Jury
   Bullion Bend robber warrants, 75–76
   Glasby witness, 75–76
Grant, James, 38-39, 42, 42f, 79, 91–92
   arrest, 43, 75
   Bullion Bend robbery expulsion, 41
   Knights of the Golden Circle (KGC) recruitment, 33, 38–39
   San Quentin sentence, 116
Grant, Ulysses S.
   Commanding General promotion, 34
   Confederacy surrender, 117
Gwin, William (Senator)
   Band of 30, 25

H
Hall, R. B. (Undersheriff), 124
   James Grant arrest, 43
   Knights of the Golden Circle (KGC) spying, 39
Hangtown, 13–14, 14f
Hodges, Frances Lundy, 17f, 33f
   Azariah Lundy, brother, 34
   children, 16, 32–34, 126, 128, 129
   death, 128
   Milpitas ranch, 32, 103

parents arrival, 128
Preston Hodges, wife, 16
Hodges, Preston, 125*f*, 126*f*
  Appeals, California Supreme Court, 107
  Bullion Bend robbery arrest, 78–79
  Bullion Bend robbery assistance, 41, 43, 72, 90
  California arrival, 16
  Captain Ingram's Partisan Rangers, 42
  conviction overturned, California Supreme Court, 112–115, 114*f*
  court case discovery, 9–10, 10*f*
  death, 130, 131*f*
  El Dorado County court trial, 88-94
  family, 32–33, 33*f*
  Frances Hodges, wife, 16, 17*f*, 128
  guilty verdict, 94
  Homestead Act application, 126, 127*f*
  illnesses, 129–130
  Lompoc Colony founding, move, 128–129
  Long Beach move, 129
  Mazatlan plans, 92
  multiple arrests post-robbery, 75-76, 125
  North Carolina cabin, 103, 104*f*
  obituary, 131
  prison record, 4*f*, 8*f*
  prison sentence, 98
  San Quentin imprisonment, 103–105, 105*f*
  Santa Clara County court charges dropped, 123–125, 124*f*
  Santa Clara County court trials, 115–116, 123
Hogan (farmer), 39
Homestead Act
  Lincoln support, 22
  Preston Hodges application, 126, 127*f*
Hopper, Art, 94
Hughey, Richard (columnist), 76, 86–87, 132
Hume, James (Undersheriff), 59, 65*f*
  biography, 71, 122
  Bullion Bend arrests, 76–78
  Bullion Bend posse, 65–66, 69, 71
  Poole interactions, 121–122
Hurlburt, S. (attorney), 80, 85, 87

I

Ingram, John, 39, 75, 78
Ingram, Rufus Henry (Red Fox), 72-76 *See also* Captain Ingram's Partisan Rangers
  Knights of the Golden Circle (KGC), 35, 35*f*, 38-39
  Quantrill's Rangers, 31–32
  stage coach driver receipt, 58, 58*f*
  mentioned in trial testimony, 87-89

J

Jarboe, Henry Ignatius, 39, 75, 78, 116
Johnson, Albert Sydney (General), 25
Johnson, James (Judge)
  El Dorado County trial critique, 120–121
  Poole letter of appeal, 121

INDEX

Jordan, Washington, 39, 75-76, 123

K
Kearney, J. G. (author), 34
Keehn, David C. (author), 19–20
Knights of the Golden Circle (KGC), 39 *See also* Captain Ingram's Partisan Rangers
    Band of 30, 3rd Degree Knights of Columbian Star, 24–25
    Bickley, founder, 19
    California control plans, 25
    California secessionists, 1861, 24
    Confederate secret society, 19–20
    Keehn description, 19–20

L
Lee, Robert E.
    offered Union command, 27
    Virginia secession, 27
Lincoln, Abraham. *See also* Civil War
    1861 assassination plot, 23–24
    assassination, 118
    California sentiments, 116–117
    post-war slavery speech, 118
    Presidential candidate, 21–24
    re-election, 108–109
Lompoc Colony
    Preston Hodges family, 128–129
    Preston Hodges founding, 128–129
Los Angeles Daily Times, 130
Low, Frederick (Governor)
    Bullion Bend robber rewards issued, 77, 77*f*
    Poole pardon requested, 120–122
Lundy, Azariah
    Frances Lundy Hodges, brother, 18
    Hodges ranch arrival, 34
Lundy, Azariah and Elizabeth (Frances parents), 128
Lundy, David, 94

M
Marin County Journal, 105
Marshall, 75–76
Marshall, James W., 13–15
Marysville Daily Appeal, 115–116
Maxey, Thomas, 94
McCallum, Ike (gang), 62, 69, 70
McClellan, George B., 109
McCracken, George, 94
McRae, Daniel, 94
McShafter, James M. (attorney), 86, 108
Militia Act of 1792, 26
Mountain Democrat
    Hughey columns, 132
    postal privileges refused, 29

N
Nevada silver discovery, 20
North Carolina cabin, Hodges, 103, 104*f*

O
Ogan, Thomas, 93
Ogan, John M., 93
Overfelt, William, 94

P
The People v. Hodges, 111
The People v. Thomas Pool, 111
Phelps, Henry, 94

Phelps, Robert M., 94
Pico Act, 20
Placerville, 79*f*, 80*f*, 81*f*. *See also* Hangtown
Placerville stagecoach robbers. *See* Captain Ingram's Partisan Rangers; Knights of the Golden Circle (KGC)
Polk, James (President), 15
Poole, Tom, 35*f*
    Appeals, California Supreme Court, 107
    Bullion Bend robbery, 55–58
    Captain Ingram's Partisan Rangers, 38, 46
    conviction remains, California Supreme Court, 111–112
    execution, 121–122
    execution order argument, Weller, 36–37
    Fort Alcatraz imprisonment, 38
    guilty verdict, 88
    hanging sentence, 97
    Hodges witness, against, 88–91
    in jail and confession, 71–72, 76, 80-82
    Knights of the Golden Circle (KGC), 35
    Somerset House injury, arrest, 62–66
    trial, 80–88
    trial witness, 89–91
Price, Sterling (General), 32

Q

Quantrill's Confederate Partisan Rangers, 31–32
    Anderson, "Bloody Bill"
    Holt, John D. (Colonel)
    James, Frank and Jesse
    Quantrill, William Clarke (Captain)
    Todd, George
    Younger, Cole

R

Ranney, George C. (Deputy Sheriff)
    Dr. Worthen and, 65
    plea for Poole, 120
    Roger's Bullion Bend posse, 58–71
    shot, Somerset House, 63
    trial testimony, 86–89
Robertson, John A., 39, 75, 78, 116, 124, 128
Robinson, John A. *See* Robertson
Rogers, William H. (Sheriff)
    Bullion Bend arrests, 76
    Bullion Bend posse, 58–71
    Bullion Bend trial testimony, 87
    Poole interactions, 121

S

Sacramento Daily Union, 122
Sacramento newspaper coverage, 78–79
San Francisco Daily Morning Call
    Mark Twain, columnist, 106
San Quentin, 103–107, 104*f*, 106*f*
Santa Clara County, trials, 114–116, 123–124
    charges dropped, 123–124, 124*f*
Santa Clara County publication
    Lincoln assassination, 119
Scott, Winfield (General), 26–27
Sherman, William Tecumseh (General), 108–109, 117
Silver discovery, Nevada, 20–21
Somerset House, 61–66, 66*f*
Stagecoach travel, 47–52, 51*f*
Staples, Joseph M.
    arrest of former suspect, 62
    Bullion Bend posse, 58–66

INDEX

death by robber, 62, 87
funeral, 67, 67f
gravestone, 68f
James Hume (friend), 65
John Dick Van Eaton (friend), 67
Sumner, Edwin (General), 25–26
Sutter's Mill, 13

T

Thomas (Judge), 116
Trials. *See* California Supreme Court, trials; El Dorado County Court, trials; Santa Clara County, trials
Twain, Mark, 21, 106

V

Van Eaton, John Dick (Deputy Sheriff)
    plea for Poole, 120
    prisoners, tricking, 71
    robbers arrests, 76–78
    Roger's Bullion Bend posse, 58–71
    trial witness, 86t, 92

W

Ward, 75
Watkins, Thomas J., 75-76
Watson, Charley, 50f
    Bullion Bend robbery and, 53–60

Bullion Bend stagecoach driver, 50, 52
Roger's Bullion Bend posse, 58-59, 69–71
trial witness, 86–89
Weller, John B. (Governor), 20
    execution order argument, Poole, 36–37
    reprieve for Anastasio, 36, 37f
Wells Fargo, 47, 48f
    Bullion Bend robber rewards, 70
    robbery loss statement, 107–108
Wilkes Booth, John, 24, 118
Williams, James W. (attorney), 81, 86, 112-113
Williams, J. J. (El Dorado County District Attorney), 86
Williams, Preston, 18
Wilson, James, 39, 116
    arrest, 75t
    Knights of the Golden Circle (KGC), 39
    robbery planning, 41, 45
    witness deal, 91–93
Worthen, H. W. A., Dr.
    El Dorado Court trial witness, 86
    Ranney treatment, 65–66

www.ingramcontent.com/pod-product-compliance
Lightning Source LLC
Chambersburg PA
CBHW071626080526
44588CB00010B/1290